The Complete
UK Air Fryer Cookbook

Easy and Flavorful Air Fryer Recipes with Step-by-Step Instructions
for Beginners and Advancers to Air Fry, Bake Every Day

Sara S. Nelson

Legal & Disclaimer

The content and information in this book is consistent and truthful, and it has been provided for informational, educational and business purposes only.

The content and information contained in this book has been compiled from reliable sources, which are accurate based on the knowledge, belief, expertise and information of the Author. The author cannot be held liable for any omissions and/ or errors.

Table of Content

Chapter 5 Fish and Seafood 29

Chapter 6 Meats 38

Chapter 7 Wraps and Sandwiches 46

Chapter 8 Appetisers and Snacks 50

Chapter 9 Desserts — 56

Chapter 10 Fast and Easy Everyday Favorites — 60

Appendix 1: Measurement Conversion Chart — 65

Appendix 2: Air Fryer Time Table — 66

Appendix 3: Recipes Index — 68

Introduction

Air fryers are the new age "must-haves" for every kitchen. They have made oil-free cooking so convenient and simple that you actually enjoy cooking at home. Due to their compact and small design, they make a perfect countertop cooking companion. With their efficient cooking technology, air fryers let you make a full menu consisting of dinners, snacks, desserts, and appetisers. And this is coming from someone who has been using air fryers for the last five years. You can always count on an air fry to cook any time of meal within just a few minutes. I have been creating several delicious meals using an air fryer, and you can do the same; all you need is a good recipe collection. Here comes a comprehensive air fryer recipe cookbook that has exciting and amazing ideas to enjoy the same old food but with lesser oil and fewer calories.

Chapter 1 Why to Air Fry?

Why do I have to go through the trouble of buying an air fry when I am already cooking food using traditional appliances? That's what most people think before making the ultimate switch! Air-frying may seem like an option, but if you closely look into the benefits of oil-free cooking, you will know that an air fryer is a good investment in the future of your health and the health of your family. By cooking food in an air fryer, you can fight all the risks of obesity, high blood cholesterol level and cardiovascular diseases. An air fryer allows you to cook healthy crispy food without using lots of cooking oil. The air frying technology consists of a heating element and a fan that blows very hot air into the cooking chamber of an air fryer. This blow of hot air actually crisps the food during cooking. According to rough estimates, compared to the results of a deep oil fryer, an air fryer can reduce your oil consumption by 70 per cent. That is not it; there are several other reasons that make an air fryer a good fit for your kitchen:

Healthy Food Every Time:

An air fryer uses less oil than a deep fryer, which is its principal health advantage. The air fryers' convection method encourages the Maillard reaction, a chemical process that results in the browning of the food. This has the benefit of making the food look better while also enhancing its flavour while having less fat.

Even Crispier Food:

Being able to cook crispy food without using oil is one of the best features of air fryers. This is accomplished by air frying food in a perforated basket or on a rack with extremely hot air from all sides, with its convection-style heating. That is why air fryers are ideal for producing crispy French fries, onion rings, fish sticks, and other conventional fried food.

Its More Efficient:

Air fryers cook food far more quickly than the majority of traditional alternative ways because of how they operate. The rapid frying method is made possible by circulating the tremendous hot air inside the fryer. Many versions either don't need to be heated up before use or only take a little time to do so. Compared to a standard oven, when you use an air fryer, the cooking time can be cut down by more than 30 to 50 per cent, depending on the particular meal.

Less Mess:

Compared to deep fryers, air fryers are much less dirty. That's because the cooking procedure only requires a small amount of oil. You don't have to set up a frying station, and there will be no splash and splatters of hot oil. The after-use cleaning is also less messy. An air fryer can be cleaned most easily with a soft-bristle brush, dishwashing soap, and some water. Air fryers retain heat inside; they don't release smoke into the air, so unlike conventional ovens, they don't raise the temperature of your kitchen.

Safer:

Air fryers are generally safer because they are self-contained appliances and because little hot oil is used in the cooking process. Splashes and burns are less of a problem. Air fryers are also designed to turn off automatically when the timer ends to avoid the food from burning. So, you can set it up to cook food and then leave it unattended without the fear of burning.

More Versatile:

An air fryer can be used to prepare most dishes that are typically cooked in a deep fryer just as well or even better. There are numerous recipes to experiment with. Surprisingly, baked items, vegetables, and steaks can all be cooked in air fryers.

Takes Lesser Space:

Kitchen appliances like air fryers are comparatively small; they are a little larger than toasters. They work well in spaces where space can be an issue, like a small kitchen. They may be kept in an RV or camper while travelling, as well as on a campsite, thanks to their compact size and lightweight.

What Should You Look for in An Air Fryer?

Buying that one air fryer that could meet all your cooking needs can be difficult since there are so many models and brands out there. As confusing as this may sound, you can still make the right decision by analysing your daily cooking needs and then look if an air fryer fits to meet those demands. Here are a few basic features that you should look into before buying an air fryer for your kitchen:

♦ Overall Size

Make sure you are aware of the amount of counter space you have first. If you frequently make chips, you might want to leave the appliance on the counter all the time. There are two varieties of air fryers, the front opening and the top opening models and depending on the space available in your kitchen; you can make the selection. Be warned that top-opening models cannot work if there isn't much room above the counter because the lid must be opened upward. If you want to store your air fryer after use, choose one that is uniform in shape and small enough to fit neatly into a cabinet.

♦ Claimed Cooking Capacity

The manufacturer's stated measurements should be taken with a grain of salt because the stated volume or capacity may be deceptive. Some manufacturers gauge the air fryer's total interior volume rather than its actual usable capacity. So while you check the cooking capacity (mentioned in litres or quartz), make sure to also check the amount of food it can accommodate.

♦ Control Panel

Dial or digital controls are the two different sorts of controls that are found in air fryers. Simpler and less precise dial controls only have a temperature dial and a timer dial that dings when the timer expires. Find a timer that can be set at an interval greater than 30 minutes. A touch display on digital controls features an accurate timer, temperature data, and in some cases, pre-programmed settings. Look for models with simple to comprehend symbols and a cooking alarm.

♦ What to Air Fry

Because air fryers use dry heat, they are excellent for roasting and baking meals. And they work well for frying without using a lot of oil as well. When air fryers initially came out, their main selling point was that they were a great appliance for cooking pre-fried frozen meals like chips, nuggets, and fish that had been battered. However, there has been a lot more experimentation in the kitchen as air fryer usage has developed and their popularity has grown.

The use of an air fryer to roast meat, bake fish and vegetables, make cakes and sweets, make granola, and roast nuts is something that supporters of the technique also boast about. Remember that air fryers quickly reach high temperatures in a limited time, so you might need to adjust cooking durations to prevent food from burning.

How to Use An Air fryer?

Similar to a wall oven in fan-forced mode, an air fryer is a small countertop cooking appliance that circulates hot, dry air to make crispy food. It is a compact cylindrical unit which comes with a removable air fryer drawer with a removable basket inside. The Air fryer has a power cord which needs to be plugged in before use. There is a control panel which has different controls depending on the type and model of the air fryer you buy. Things that you can control with this panel are mainly the cooking time and temperature.

To get started with your air frying experience, first, place the air fryer on a sturdy surface near a power outlet and 4-5 inches away from other appliances and surfaces while using it. Plug it in and switch it on. Most air fryers require 3-5 minutes of preheating, and you can do it before or after adding the food to its basket. Pull the air fryer drawer and place the food in its basket, then slide the drawer back in. There are accessories like a baking pan, cooking rack and small ramekins that you can also place inside the air fryer basket to cook all sorts of food. To air fry the food inside, simple set the cooking time and temperature as per the given instructions in the recipe. If your air fryer has its own preset, then follow the user manual to adjust the settings accordingly. The device initiates cooking after preheating, and it beeps or indicates when the food is done. It is best to check the food 5 minutes before the completion of the actual cooking cycle to avoid overcooking.

To ensure even cooking, air fryers with a pull-out drawer and basket need to be manually shaken roughly every five minutes or halfway through the entire cooking time. You'll need to make an effort to remember this yourself since the majority of models lack a timer or alarm to remind you to shake or flip your meal. The models with such a flip or shake reminder work best for meals like fish, poultry, meatballs, vegetables, and crumbed dishes.

Cleaning An Air Fryer

You'll regret waiting to clean; don't put it off. If you leave the food leftovers and crumbs in the basket and drawer overnight, it will be challenging to clean them later. Unplug the air fryer after frying is finished, let it cool, then remove the oil from the pull-out drawer and throw it away.

After air-frying items covered in a sticky sauce, like marinated ribs, wipe the grate, basket, and drawer while the surfaces are still heated. This will allow clearing the gunk easier. Wash the leftover food pieces with warm, soapy water. Use a soft towel or sponge instead of abrasives to clean. In order to clean any pieces that have food adhered to them, soak them in hot water with dish soap to dissolve the food.

Use a wooden skewer or toothpick to free any food that may be lodged in the grate or basket. Each component needs to be dried separately. To clean the inside of the air fryer, use a wet towel bathed in warm, soapy water. The drawer and basket must nevertheless be removed. Check for grease and food crumbs before cleaning the heating element. Some manufacturers caution against removing food that has stuck to surfaces with steel wire. Reassemble after drying. Wipe the exterior of the item with a damp cloth or sponge, then dry it.

To get rid of the after-cook smell left inside the air fryer basket, both the basket and drawer should be soaked in soapy water for 30 to 60 minutes before cleaning again. If the odour still exists, cut a lemon in half, rub it over the basket and drawer, and then rewash after 30 minutes.

While cleaning the air fryer, make sure never to immerse the unit in liquid or don't pour the liquid over it. Keep the air fryer's power cord away from hot surfaces. Avoid scrubbing the interior or exterior surfaces of the air fryer with hard steel or any sharp object, as that may cause damage.

FAQs about Air Fryer

1. Do I have to add oil to the food for air frying?

When you are using an air fryer, you only need up to 1 tablespoon of oil for every kilogramme of fresh food. Although oil gives food flavour, it is not necessary for cooking pre-cooked frozen items. You can use an oil mister to add a light layer of oil over the food. This light layer is only there to prevent the food from completely drying out during cooking.

2. Can I reheat the cooked in an air fryer?

Reheating food in air fryers is excellent if you want to preserve its crispiness and avoid making it mushy, such as with pizza and items that have been battered. These days most new air fryers come with a "reheat" preset which is perfect for doing so. If there is no such preset, then simply set the temperature to 325 degrees F and reheat the food for 3-5 minutes.

3. In an air fryer, how many chips can I make?

Depending on the cooking capacity of an air fryer, you can cook between 1 lb. and 2 lbs. of chips, which is plenty for 2-4 people.

4. Can I use foil and baking paper in an air fryer?

Before using foil or baking paper in your air fryer, always verify the manufacturer's instructions. Although it is conceivable, you should exercise caution and think about how it can affect the final product. Because covering the bottom of the basket with baking paper or foil could disrupt and reduce airflow, affecting cooking performance, several manufacturers advise against doing so.

Conclusion

With an air fryer, you may prepare your complete day's worth of food in just one place. Use the extensive range of recipes offered in this cookbook if you have an air fryer at home. You may prepare everything in your air fryer, from nutritious lunches, snacks, dinners, and desserts. Each recipe is equipped with general and simple-to-follow instructions, which can be used for any air fryer. Since each air fryer has its own control panel with particular features, you must use the temperature and time settings of the recipes in accordance with the user manual that comes with your appliance. Have a happy air-frying experience!

Chapter 2 Breakfasts

PB&J

Prep time: 5 minutes | Cook time: 6 minutes | Serves 4

25 g cornflakes, crushed
20 g desiccated coconut
8 slices oat nut bread or any whole-grain, oversize bread
6 tbsps. peanut butter
2 medium bananas, cut into 1-cm thick slices
6 tbsps. pineapple preserves
1 egg, beaten
Cooking spray

1. Preheat the air fryer to 180ºC.
2. In a shallow dish, mix the cornflake crumbs and coconut.
3. For each sandwich, spread one bread slice with 1½ tbsps. of peanut butter. Top with banana slices. Spread another bread slice with 1½ tbsps. of preserves. Combine to make a sandwich.
4. Using a pastry brush, brush top of sandwich lightly with beaten egg. Sprinkle with about 1½ tbsps. of crumb coating, pressing it in to make it stick. Spray with cooking spray.
5. Turn sandwich over and repeat to coat and spray the other side.
6. Air frying 2 at a time, place sandwiches in air fryer basket and air fry for 6 minutes or until coating is golden brown and crispy.
7. Cut the cooked sandwiches in half and serve warm.

Buttermilk Biscuits

Prep time: 5 minutes | Cook time: 5 minutes | Makes 12 biscuits

250 g plain flour, plus more for dusting the work surface
1 tbsp. baking powder
¼ tsp. baking soda
2 tsps. sugar
1 tsp. salt
6 tbsps. cold unsalted butter, cut into 1-tbsp. slices
180 ml buttermilk

1. Preheat the air fryer to 180ºC. Spray the air fryer basket with olive oil.
2. In a large mixing bowl, combine the flour, baking powder, baking soda, sugar, and salt and mix well.
3. Using a fork, cut in the butter until the mixture resembles coarse meal.
4. Add the buttermilk and mix until smooth.
5. Dust more flour on a clean work surface. Turn the dough out onto the work surface and roll it out until it is about 1 cm thick.
6. Using a 4-cm biscuit cutter, cut out the biscuits. Put the uncooked biscuits in the greased air fryer basket in a single layer.
7. Bake for 5 minutes. Transfer the cooked biscuits from the air fryer to a platter.
8. Cut the remaining biscuits. Bake the remaining biscuits.
9. Serve warm.

Classic British Breakfast

Prep time: 5 minutes | Cook time: 25 minutes | Serves 2

140 g potatoes, sliced and diced
200 g beans in tomato sauce
2 eggs
1 tbsp. olive oil
1 sausage
Salt, to taste

1. Preheat the air fryer to 200ºC and allow to warm.
2. Break the eggs onto a baking dish and sprinkle with salt.
3. Lay the beans on the dish, next to the eggs.
4. In a bowl, coat the potatoes with the olive oil. Sprinkle with salt.
5. Transfer the bowl of potato slices to the air fryer and bake for 10 minutes.
6. Swap out the bowl of potatoes for the dish containing the eggs and beans. Bake for another 10 minutes. Cover the potatoes with parchment paper.
7. Slice up the sausage and throw the slices on top of the beans and eggs. Bake for another 5 minutes.
8. Serve with the potatoes.

Mushroom and Squash Toast

Prep time: 10 minutes | Cook time: 10 minutes | Serves 4

1 tbsp. olive oil
1 red pepper, cut into strips
2 spring onions, sliced
88 g sliced button or cremini mushrooms
1 small yellow squash, sliced
2 tbsps. softened butter
4 slices bread
110 g soft goat cheese

1. Brush the air fryer basket with the olive oil and preheat the air fryer to 180ºC.
2. Put the red pepper, spring onions, mushrooms, and squash inside the air fryer, give them a stir and air fry for 7 minutes or the vegetables are tender, shaking the basket once throughout the cooking time.
3. Remove the vegetables and set them aside.
4. Spread the butter on the slices of bread and transfer to the air fryer, butter-side up. Brown for 3 minutes.
5. Remove the toast from the air fryer and top with goat cheese and vegetables. Serve warm.

Onion Omelet

Prep time: 10 minutes | Cook time: 12 minutes | Serves 2

3 eggs
Salt and ground black pepper, to taste
½ tsps. soy sauce
1 large onion, chopped
2 tbsps. grated Cheddar cheese
Cooking spray

1. Preheat the air fryer to 180ºC.
2. In a bowl, whisk together the eggs, salt, pepper, and soy sauce.
3. Spritz a small pan with cooking spray. Spread the chopped onion across the bottom of the pan, then transfer the pan to the air fryer.
4. Bake in the preheated air fryer for 6 minutes or until the onion is translucent.
5. Add the egg mixture on top of the onions to coat well. Add the cheese on top, then continue baking for another 6 minutes.
6. Allow to cool before serving.

English Pumpkin Egg Bake

Prep time: 10 minutes | Cook time: 10 minutes | Serves 2

2 eggs
120 ml milk
250 g flour
2 tbsps. cider vinegar
2 tsps. baking powder
1 tbsp. sugar
230 g pumpkin purée
1 tsp. cinnamon powder
1 tsp. baking soda
1 tbsp. olive oil

1. Preheat the air fryer to 150ºC.
2. Crack the eggs into a bowl and beat with a whisk. Combine with the milk, flour, cider vinegar, baking powder, sugar, pumpkin purée, cinnamon powder, and baking soda, mixing well.
3. Grease a baking tray with oil. Add the mixture and transfer into the air fryer. Bake for 10 minutes.
4. Serve warm.

Parmesan Ranch Risotto

Prep time: 10 minutes | Cook time: 30 minutes | Serves 2

1 tbsp. olive oil
1 clove garlic, minced
1 tbsp. unsalted butter
1 onion, diced

150 g Arborio rice
450 ml chicken stock, boiling
45 g Parmesan cheese, grated

1. Preheat the air fryer to 200ºC.
2. Grease a round baking tin with olive oil and stir in the garlic, butter, and onion.
3. Transfer the tin to the air fryer and bake for 4 minutes. Add the rice and bake for 4 more minutes.
4. Turn the air fryer to 160ºC and pour in the chicken stock. Cover and bake for 22 minutes.
5. Scatter with cheese and serve.

Banana Churros with Oatmeal

Prep time: 15 minutes | Cook time: 15 minutes | Serves 2

For the Churros:
1 large yellow banana, peeled, cut in half lengthwise, then cut in half widthwise
2 tbsps. whole-wheat pastry flour
⅛ tsp. sea salt
2 tsps. oil (sunflower or melted coconut)
1 tsp. water

Cooking spray
1 tbsp. coconut sugar
½ tsp. cinnamon
For the Oatmeal:
120 g rolled oats
360 ml water

To make the churros:
1. Put the 4 banana pieces in a medium-size bowl and add the flour and salt. Stir gently. Add the oil and water. Stir gently until evenly mixed. You may need to press some coating onto the banana pieces.
2. Spray the air fryer basket with the oil spray. Put the banana pieces in the air fryer basket and air fry for 5 minutes. Remove, gently turn over, and air fry for another 5 minutes or until browned.
3. In a medium bowl, add the coconut sugar and cinnamon and stir to combine. When the banana pieces are nicely browned, spray with the oil and place in the cinnamon-sugar bowl. Toss gently with a spatula to coat the banana pieces with the mixture.
To make the oatmeal:
4. While the bananas are cooking, make the oatmeal. In a medium pot, bring the oats and water to a boil, then reduce to low heat. Simmer, stirring often, until all the water is absorbed, about 5 minutes. Put the oatmeal into two bowls.
5. Top the oatmeal with the coated banana pieces and serve immediately.

Simple Scotch Eggs

Prep time: 5 minutes | Cook time: 25 minutes | Serves 4

4 large hard boiled eggs
1 (340-g) package pork sausage
8 slices thick-cut bacon

Special Equipment:
4 wooden toothpicks, soaked in water for at least 30 minutes

1. Slice the sausage into four parts and place each part into a large circle.
2. Put an egg into each circle and wrap it in the sausage. Put in the refrigerator for 1 hour.
3. Preheat the air fryer to 235ºC.
4. Make a cross with two pieces of thick-cut bacon. Put a wrapped egg in the centre, fold the bacon over top of the egg, and secure with a toothpick.
5. Air fry in the preheated air fryer for 25 minutes.
6. Serve immediately.

Chapter 3 Vegetables

Creamy and Cheesy Spinach

Prep time: 10 minutes | Cook time: 15 minutes | Serves 4

Vegetable oil spray
1 (283-g) package frozen spinach, thawed and squeezed dry
30 g chopped onion
2 cloves garlic, minced
113 g cream cheese, diced
½ tsp. ground nutmeg
1 tsp. salt
1 tsp. black pepper
47 g grated Parmesan cheese

1. Preheat the air fryer to 180ºC. Spray a heatproof pan with vegetable oil spray.
2. In a medium bowl, combine the spinach, onion, garlic, cream cheese, nutmeg, salt, and pepper. Transfer to the prepared pan.
3. Put the pan in the air fryer basket. Bake for 10 minutes. Open and stir to thoroughly combine the cream cheese and spinach.
4. Sprinkle the Parmesan cheese on top. Bake for 5 minutes, or until the cheese has melted and browned.
5. Serve hot.

Blistered Shishito Peppers

Prep time: 10 minutes | Cook time: 6 minutes | Serves 4

Dipping Sauce:
245 g sour cream
2 tbsps. fresh lemon juice
1 clove garlic, minced
1 spring onion (white and green parts), finely chopped
Peppers:
227 g shishito peppers
1 tbsp. vegetable oil
1 tsp. toasted sesame oil
Salt and black pepper, to taste
¼ to ½ tsp. red pepper flakes
½ tsp. toasted sesame seeds

1. In a small bowl, stir all the ingredients for the dipping sauce to combine. Cover and refrigerate until serving time.
2. Preheat the air fryer to 200ºC.
3. In a medium bowl, toss the peppers with the vegetable oil. Put the peppers in the air fryer basket. Air fry for 6 minutes, or until peppers are lightly charred in spots, stirring the peppers halfway through the cooking time.
4. Transfer the peppers to a serving bowl. Drizzle with the sesame oil and toss to coat. Season with salt and pepper. Sprinkle with the red pepper and sesame seeds and toss again.
5. Serve immediately with the dipping sauce

Golden Pickles

Prep time: 10 minutes | Cook time: 15 minutes | Serves 4

14 dill pickles, sliced
30 g flour
⅛ tsp. baking powder
Pinch of salt
2 tbsps. cornflour plus 3 tbsps. water
6 tbsps. panko bread crumbs
½ tsp. paprika
Cooking spray

1. Preheat the air fryer to 200ºC.
2. Drain any excess moisture out of the dill pickles on a paper towel.
3. In a bowl, combine the flour, baking powder and salt.
4. Throw in the cornflour and water mixture and combine well with a whisk.
5. Put the panko bread crumbs in a shallow dish along with the paprika. Mix thoroughly.
6. Dip the pickles in the flour batter, before coating in the bread crumbs. Spritz all the pickles with the cooking spray.
7. Transfer to the air fryer basket and air fry for 15 minutes, or until golden brown.
8. Serve immediately.

Cauliflower Tater Tots

Prep time: 15 minutes | Cook time: 16 minutes | Serves 12

454 g cauliflower, steamed and chopped
120 g nutritional yeast
1 tbsp. oats
1 tbsp. desiccated coconuts
3 tbsps. flaxseed meal
3 tbsps. water
1 onion, chopped
1 tsp. minced garlic
1 tsp. chopped parsley
1 tsp. chopped oregano
1 tsp. chopped chives
Salt and ground black pepper, to taste
60 g bread crumbs

1. Preheat the air fryer to 200ºC.
2. Drain any excess water out of the cauliflower by wringing it with a paper towel.
3. In a bowl, combine the cauliflower with the remaining ingredients, save the bread crumbs. Using the hands, shape the mixture into several small balls.
4. Coat the balls in the bread crumbs and transfer to the air fryer basket. Air fry for 6 minutes, then raise the temperature to 204ºC and then air fry for an additional 10 minutes.
5. Serve immediately.

Easy Potato Croquettes

Prep time: 15 minutes | Cook time: 15 minutes | Serves 10

60 g nutritional yeast
300 g boiled potatoes, mashed
1 flax egg
1 tbsp. flour
2 tbsps. chopped chives
Salt and ground black pepper, to taste
2 tbsps. vegetable oil
30 g breadcrumbs

1. Preheat the air fryer to 200ºC.
2. In a bowl, combine the nutritional yeast, potatoes, flax egg, flour, and chives. Sprinkle with salt and pepper as desired.
3. In a separate bowl, mix the vegetable oil and bread crumbs to achieve a crumbly consistency.
4. Shape the potato mixture into small balls and dip each one into the breadcrumb mixture.
5. Put the croquettes inside the air fryer and air fry for 15 minutes, ensuring the croquettes turn golden brown.
6. Serve immediately.

Spicy Cauliflower Roast

Prep time: 15 minutes | Cook time: 20 minutes | Serves 4

Cauliflower:
563 g cauliflower florets
3 tbsps. vegetable oil
½ tsp. ground cumin
½ tsp. ground coriander
½ tsp. salt
Sauce:
150 g Greek yogurt or sour cream
15 g chopped fresh coriander
1 jalapeño, coarsely chopped
4 cloves garlic, peeled
½ tsp. salt
2 tbsps. water

1. Preheat the air fryer to 200ºC.
2. In a large bowl, combine the cauliflower, oil, cumin, coriander, and salt. Toss to coat.
3. Put the cauliflower in the air fryer basket. Roast for 20 minutes, stirring halfway through the roasting time.
4. Meanwhile, in a blender, combine the yogurt, coriander, jalapeño, garlic, and salt. Blend, adding the water as needed to keep the blades moving and to thin the sauce.
5. At the end of roasting time, transfer the cauliflower to a large serving bowl. Pour the sauce over and toss gently to coat. Serve immediately.

Golden Garlicky Mushrooms

Prep time: 10 minutes | Cook time: 10 minutes | Serves 4

6 small mushrooms
1 tbsp. bread crumbs
1 tbsp. olive oil
28 g onion, peeled and diced

1 tsp. parsley
1 tsp. garlic purée
Salt and ground black pepper, to taste

1. Preheat the air fryer to 180ºC.
2. Combine the bread crumbs, oil, onion, parsley, salt, pepper and garlic in a bowl. Cut out the mushrooms' stalks and stuff each cap with the crumb mixture.
3. Air fry in the air fryer for 10 minutes.
4. Serve hot.

Lush Vegetable Salad

Prep time: 15 minutes | Cook time: 10 minutes | Serves 4

6 plum tomatoes, halved
2 large red onions, sliced
4 long red pepper, sliced
2 yellow pepper, sliced
6 cloves garlic, crushed

1 tbsp. extra-virgin olive oil
1 tsp. paprika
½ lemon, juiced
Salt and ground black pepper, to taste
1 tbsp. baby capers

1. Preheat the air fryer to 220ºC.
2. Put the tomatoes, onions, peppers, and garlic in a large bowl and cover with the extra-virgin olive oil, paprika, and lemon juice. Sprinkle with salt and pepper as desired.
3. Line the inside of the air fryer basket with aluminum foil. Put the vegetables inside and air fry for 10 minutes, ensuring the edges turn brown.
4. Serve in a salad bowl with the baby capers.

Sweet and Sour Tofu

Prep time: 15 minutes | Cook time: 20 minutes | Serves 2

2 tsps. apple cider vinegar
1 tbsp. sugar
1 tbsp. soy sauce
3 tsps. lime juice
1 tsp. ground ginger
1 tsp. garlic powder

½ block firm tofu, pressed to remove excess liquid and cut into cubes
1 tsp. cornflour
2 spring onions, chopped
Toasted sesame seeds, for garnish

1. In a bowl, thoroughly combine the apple cider vinegar, sugar, soy sauce, lime juice, ground ginger, and garlic powder.
2. Cover the tofu with this mixture and leave to marinate for at least 30 minutes.
3. Preheat the air fryer to 200ºC.
4. Transfer the tofu to the air fryer, keeping any excess marinade for the sauce. Air fry for 20 minutes or until crispy.
5. In the meantime, thicken the sauce with the cornflour over a medium-low heat.
6. Serve the cooked tofu with the sauce, spring onions, and sesame seeds.

Air Fried Potatoes with Olives

Prep time: 15 minutes | Cook time: 40 minutes | Serves 1

1 medium russet potatoes, scrubbed and peeled
1 tsp. olive oil
¼ tsp. onion powder
⅛ tsp. salt

Dollop of butter
Dollop of cream cheese
1 tbsp. Kalamata olives
1 tbsp. chopped chives

1. Preheat the air fryer to 200ºC.
2. In a bowl, coat the potatoes with the onion powder, salt, olive oil, and butter.
3. Transfer to the air fryer and air fry for 40 minutes, turning the potatoes over at the halfway point.
4. Take care when removing the potatoes from the air fryer and serve with the cream cheese, Kalamata olives and chives on top.

Marinara Pepperoni Mushroom Pizza

Prep time: 5 minutes | Cook time: 18 minutes | Serves 4

4 large portobello mushrooms, stems removed
4 tsps. olive oil
235 g marinara sauce

160 g shredded Mozzarella cheese
10 slices sugar-free pepperoni

1. Preheat the air fryer to 190ºC.
2. Brush each mushroom cap with the olive oil, one tsp. for each cap.
3. Put on a baking sheet and bake, stem-side down, for 8 minutes.
4. Take out of the air fryer and divide the marinara sauce, Mozzarella cheese and pepperoni evenly among the caps.
5. Air fry for another 10 minutes until browned.
6. Serve hot.

Chermoula Beetroot Roast

Prep time: 15 minutes | Cook time: 25 minutes | Serves 4

Chermoula:
50 g packed fresh coriander leaves
25 g packed fresh parsley leaves
6 cloves garlic, peeled
2 tsps. smoked paprika
2 tsps. ground cumin
1 tsp. ground coriander
½ to 1 tsp. cayenne pepper

Pinch of crushed saffron (optional)
120 ml extra-virgin olive oil
Salt, to taste
Beetroot:
3 medium beetroot, trimmed, peeled, and cut into
2-cm chunks
2 tbsps. chopped fresh coriander
2 tbsps. chopped fresh parsley

1. In a food processor, combine the coriander, parsley, garlic, paprika, cumin, coriander, and cayenne. Pulse until coarsely chopped. Add the saffron, if using, and process until combined. With the food processor running, slowly add the olive oil in a steady stream; process until the sauce is uniform. Season with salt.
2. Preheat the air fryer to 190ºC.
3. In a large bowl, drizzle the beets with ½ cup of the chermoula to coat. Arrange the beets in the air fryer basket. Roast for 25 to minutes, or until the beets are tender.
4. Transfer the beets to a serving platter. Sprinkle with the chopped coriander and parsley and serve.

Air Fried Asparagus

Prep time: 5 minutes | Cook time: 5 minutes | Serves 4

454 g fresh asparagus spears, trimmed
1 tbsp. olive oil

Salt and ground black pepper, to taste

1. Preheat the air fryer to 190ºC.
2. Combine all the ingredients and transfer to the air fryer basket.
3. Air fry for 5 minutes or until soft.
4. Serve hot.

Jalapeño Poppers

Prep time: 5 minutes | Cook time: 33 minutes | Serves 4

8 medium jalapeño peppers
142 g cream cheese
60 g grated Mozzarella cheese

½ tsp. Italian seasoning mix
8 slices bacon

1. Preheat the air fryer to 200ºC.
2. Cut the jalapeños in half.
3. Use a spoon to scrape out the insides of the peppers.
4. In a bowl, add together the cream cheese, Mozzarella cheese and Italian seasoning.
5. Pack the cream cheese mixture into the jalapeño halves and place the other halves on top.
6. Wrap each pepper in 1 slice of bacon, starting from the bottom and working up.
7. Bake for 33 minutes.
8. Serve!

Mascarpone Mushrooms

Prep time: 10 minutes | Cook time: 15 minutes | Serves 4

Vegetable oil spray
423 g sliced mushrooms
1 medium yellow onion, chopped
2 cloves garlic, minced
63 g heavy whipping cream
227 g mascarpone cheese

1 tsp. dried thyme
1 tsp. salt
1 tsp. black pepper
½ tsp. red pepper flakes
634 g cooked konjac noodles, for serving
30 g grated Parmesan cheese

1. Preheat the air fryer to 180ºC. Spray a heatproof pan with vegetable oil spray.
2. In a medium bowl, combine the mushrooms, onion, garlic, cream, mascarpone, thyme, salt, black pepper, and red pepper flakes. Stir to combine. Transfer the mixture to the prepared pan.
3. Put the pan in the air fryer basket. Bake for 15 minutes, stirring halfway through the baking time.
4. Divide the pasta among four shallow bowls. Spoon the mushroom mixture evenly over the pasta. Sprinkle with Parmesan cheese and serve.

Lemony Falafel

Prep time: 15 minutes | Cook time: 15 minutes | Serves 8

1 tsp. cumin seeds
½ tsp. coriander seeds
350 g chickpeas, drained and rinsed
½ tsp. red pepper flakes
3 cloves garlic
15 g chopped parsley

15 g chopped coriander
½ onion, diced
1 tbsp. juice from freshly squeezed lemon
3 tbsps. flour
½ tsp. salt
Cooking spray

1. Fry the cumin and coriander seeds over medium heat until fragrant.
2. Grind using a mortar and pestle.
3. Put all of ingredients, except for the cooking spray, in a food processor and blend until a fine consistency is achieved.
4. Use the hands to mold the mixture into falafels and spritz with the cooking spray.
5. Preheat the air fryer to 200ºC.
6. Transfer the falafels to the air fryer basket in one layer.
7. Air fry for 15 minutes, serving when they turn golden brown.

Chapter 4 Poultry

Merguez Meatballs

Prep time: 10 minutes | Cook time: 10 minutes | Serves 4

454 g chicken mince
2 garlic cloves, finely minced
1 tbsp. sweet Hungarian paprika
1 tsp. salt
1 tsp. sugar
1 tsp. ground cumin
½ tsp. black pepper
½ tsp. ground fennel
½ tsp. ground coriander
½ tsp. cayenne pepper
¼ tsp. ground allspice

1. In a large bowl, gently mix the chicken, garlic, paprika, salt, sugar, cumin, black pepper, fennel, coriander, cayenne, and allspice until all the ingredients are incorporated. Let stand for 30 minutes at room temperature, or cover and refrigerate for up to 24 hours.
2. Preheat the air fryer to 200ºC.
3. Form the mixture into 16 meatballs. Arrange them in a single layer in the air fryer basket. Air fry for 10 minutes, turning the meatballs halfway through the cooking time. Use a meat thermometer to ensure the meatballs have reached an internal temperature of 75ºC.
4. Serve warm.

Cheesy Chicken Tacos

Prep time: 10 minutes | Cook time: 12 to 16 minutes | Serves 2 to 4

1 tsp. chili powder
½ tsp. ground cumin
½ tsp. garlic powder
Salt and pepper, to taste
Pinch cayenne pepper
454 g boneless, skinless chicken thighs, trimmed
1 tsp. vegetable oil
1 tomato, cored and chopped
2 tbsps. finely chopped red onion
2 tsps. minced jalapeño chili
1½ tsps. lime juice
6 to 12 (12-cm) corn tortillas, warmed
60 g shredded iceberg lettuce
85 g cheddar cheese, shredded

1. Preheat the air fryer to 200ºC.
2. Combine chili powder, cumin, garlic powder, ½ tsp. salt, ¼ tsp. pepper, and cayenne in bowl. Pat chicken dry with paper towels, rub with oil, and sprinkle evenly with spice mixture. Place chicken in air fryer basket. Air fry until chicken registers 75ºC, 12 to 16 minutes, flipping chicken halfway through cooking.
3. Meanwhile, combine tomato, onion, jalapeño, and lime juice in a bowl; season with salt and pepper to taste and set aside until ready to serve.
4. Transfer chicken to a cutting board, let cool slightly, then shred into bite-size pieces using 2 forks. Serve chicken on warm tortillas, topped with salsa, lettuce, and cheddar.

Simple Chicken Shawarma

Prep time: 10 minutes | Cook time: 15 minutes | Serves 4

Shawarma Spice:
2 tsps. dried oregano
1 tsp. ground cinnamon
1 tsp. ground cumin
1 tsp. ground coriander
1 tsp. salt
½ tsp. ground allspice
½ tsp. cayenne pepper
Chicken:
454 g boneless, skinless chicken thighs, cut into large bite-size chunks
2 tbsps. vegetable oil
For Serving:
Tzatziki
Pita bread

1. For the shawarma spice: In a small bowl, combine the oregano, cayenne, cumin, coriander, salt, cinnamon, and allspice.
2. For the chicken: In a large bowl, toss together the chicken, vegetable oil, and shawarma spice to coat. Marinate at room temperature for 30 minutes or cover and refrigerate for up to 24 hours.
3. Preheat the air fryer to 180ºC. Place the chicken in the air fryer basket. Air fry for 15 minutes, or until the chicken reaches an internal temperature of 75ºC.
4. Transfer the chicken to a serving platter. Serve with tzatziki and pita bread.

Barbecued Chicken with Creamy Coleslaw

Prep time: 10 minutes | Cook time: 20 minutes | Serves 2

80 g shredded coleslaw mix
Salt and pepper
2 (340-g) bone-in split chicken breasts, trimmed
1 tsp. vegetable oil
2 tbsps. barbecue sauce, plus extra for serving
2 tbsps. mayonnaise
2 tbsps. sour cream
1 tsp. distilled white vinegar, plus extra for seasoning
¼ tsp. sugar

1. Preheat the air fryer to 180ºC.
2. Toss coleslaw mix and ¼ tsp. salt in a colander set over bowl. Let sit until wilted slightly, about 30 minutes. Rinse, drain, and dry well with a dish towel.
3. Meanwhile, pat chicken dry with paper towels, rub with oil, and season with salt and pepper. Arrange breasts skin-side down in air fryer basket, spaced evenly apart, alternating ends. Bake for 10 minutes. Flip breasts and brush skin side with barbecue sauce. Return basket to air fryer and bake until well browned and chicken registers 70ºC, 10 to 15 minutes.
4. Transfer chicken to serving platter, tent loosely with aluminum foil, and let rest for 5 minutes. While chicken rests, whisk mayonnaise, sour cream, vinegar, sugar, and pinch pepper together in a large bowl. Stir in coleslaw mix and season with salt, pepper, and additional vinegar to taste. Serve chicken with coleslaw, passing extra barbecue sauce separately.

Crisp Chicken Wings

Prep time: 15 minutes | Cook time: 20 minutes | Serves 4

454 g chicken wings
3 tbsps. vegetable oil
62 g plain flour
½ tsp. smoked paprika
½ tsp. garlic powder
½ tsp. salt
1½ tsps. freshly cracked black pepper

1. Preheat the air fryer to 200ºC.
2. Place the chicken wings in a large bowl. Drizzle the vegetable oil over wings and toss to coat.
3. In a separate bowl, whisk together the flour, paprika, garlic powder, salt, and pepper until combined.
4. Dredge the wings in the flour mixture one at a time, coating them well, and place in the air fryer basket. Air fry for 20 minutes, turning the wings halfway through the cooking time, until the breading is browned and crunchy.
5. Serve hot.

Herb-Buttermilk Chicken Breast

Prep time: 5 minutes | Cook time: 40 minutes | Serves 2

1 large bone-in, skin-on chicken breast
240 ml buttermilk
1½ tsps. dried parsley
1½ tsps. dried chives
¾ tsp. salt
½ tsp. dried dill
½ tsp. onion powder
¼ tsp. garlic powder
¼ tsp. dried tarragon
Cooking spray

1. Place the chicken breast in a bowl and pour over the buttermilk, turning the chicken in it to make sure it's completely covered. Let the chicken stand at room temperature for at least 20 minutes or in the refrigerator for up to 4 hours.
2. Meanwhile, in a bowl, stir together the parsley, chives, salt, dill, onion powder, garlic powder, and tarragon.
3. Preheat the air fryer to 150ºC.
4. Remove the chicken from the buttermilk, letting the excess drip off, then place the chicken skin-side up directly in the air fryer. Sprinkle the seasoning mix all over the top of the chicken breast, then let stand until the herb mix soaks into the buttermilk, at least 5 minutes.
5. Spray the top of the chicken with cooking spray. Bake for 10 minutes, then increase the temperature to 180ºC and bake until an instant-read thermometer inserted into the thickest part of the breast reads 70ºC and the chicken is deep golden brown, 30 to 35 minutes.
6. Transfer the chicken breast to a cutting board, let rest for 10 minutes, then cut the meat off the bone and cut into thick slices for serving.

Paprika Indian Fennel Chicken

Prep time: 10 minutes | Cook time: 15 minutes | Serves 4

454 g boneless, skinless chicken thighs, cut crosswise into thirds
1 yellow onion, cut into 3-cm thick slices
1 tbsp. coconut oil, melted
2 tsps. minced fresh ginger
2 tsps. minced garlic
1 tsp. smoked paprika
1 tsp. ground fennel

1 tsp. garam masala
1 tsp. ground turmeric
1 tsp. salt
½ to 1 tsp. cayenne pepper
Vegetable oil spray
2 tsps. fresh lemon juice
15 g chopped fresh coriander or parsley

1. Use a fork to pierce the chicken all over to allow the marinade to penetrate better.
2. In a large bowl, combine the onion, coconut oil, ginger, garlic, paprika, fennel, garam masala, turmeric, salt, and cayenne. Add the chicken, toss to combine, and marinate at room temperature for 30 minutes, or cover and refrigerate for up to 24 hours.
3. Preheat the air fryer to 180ºC.
4. Place the chicken and onion in the air fryer basket. (Discard remaining marinade.) Spray with some vegetable oil spray. Air fry for 15 minutes. Halfway through the cooking time, remove the basket, spray the chicken and onion with more vegetable oil spray, and toss gently to coat. At the end of the cooking time, use a meat thermometer to ensure the chicken has reached an internal temperature of 75ºC.
5. Transfer the chicken and onion to a serving platter. Sprinkle with the lemon juice and coriander and serve.

Hawaiian Tropical Chicken

Prep time: 10 minutes | Cook time: 15 minutes | Serves 4

4 boneless, skinless chicken thighs (680 g)
1 (227-g) can pineapple chunks in juice, drained, 60 ml juice reserved
60 ml soy sauce
50 g sugar

2 tbsps. ketchup
1 tbsp. minced fresh ginger
1 tbsp. minced garlic
15 g chopped spring onions

1. Use a fork to pierce the chicken all over to allow the marinade to penetrate better. Place the chicken in a large bowl or large resealable plastic bag.
2. Set the drained pineapple chunks aside. In a small microwave-safe bowl, combine the pineapple juice, soy sauce, sugar, ketchup, ginger, and garlic. Pour half the sauce over the chicken; toss to coat. Reserve the remaining sauce. Marinate the chicken at room temperature for 30 minutes, or cover and refrigerate for up to 24 hours.
3. Preheat the air fryer to 180ºC.
4. Place the chicken in the air fryer basket, discarding marinade. Bake for 15 minutes, turning halfway through the cooking time.
5. Meanwhile, microwave the reserved sauce on high for 45 to 60 seconds, stirring every 15 seconds, until the sauce has the consistency of a thick glaze.
6. At the end of the cooking time, use a meat thermometer to ensure the chicken has reached an internal temperature of 75C.
7. Transfer the chicken to a serving platter. Pour the sauce over the chicken. Garnish with the pineapple chunks and spring onions before serving.

Thai Curry Meatballs

Prep time: 10 minutes | Cook time: 10 minutes | Serves 4

454 g chicken mince
15 g chopped fresh coriander
1 tsp. chopped fresh mint
1 tbsp. fresh lime juice
1 tbsp. Thai red, green, or yellow curry paste
1 tbsp. fish sauce

2 garlic cloves, minced
2 tsps. minced fresh ginger
½ tsp. salt
½ tsp. black pepper
¼ tsp. red pepper flakes

1. Preheat the air fryer to 200ºC.
2. In a large bowl, gently mix the chicken mince, coriander, mint, lime juice, curry paste, fish sauce, garlic, ginger, salt, black pepper, and red pepper flakes until thoroughly combined.
3. Form the mixture into 16 meatballs. Place the meatballs in a single layer in the air fryer basket. Air fry for 10 minutes, turning the meatballs halfway through the cooking time. Use a meat thermometer to ensure the meatballs have reached an internal temperature of 75ºC. Serve immediately.

Parmesan Chicken Wings

Prep time: 15 minutes | Cook time: 16 to 18 minutes | Serves 4

112 g grated Parmesan cheese
1 tbsp. garlic powder
1 tsp. salt
½ tsp. freshly ground black pepper

95 g plain flour
1 large egg, beaten
12 chicken wings (454 g)
Cooking spray

1. Preheat the air fryer to 200ºC. Line the air fryer basket with parchment paper.
2. In a shallow bowl, whisk the Parmesan cheese, garlic powder, salt, and pepper until blended. Place the flour in a second shallow bowl and the beaten egg in a third shallow bowl.
3. One at a time, dip the chicken wings into the flour, the beaten egg, and the Parmesan cheese mixture, coating thoroughly.
4. Place the chicken wings on the parchment and spritz with cooking spray.
5. Air fry for 8 minutes. Flip the chicken, spritz it with cooking spray, and air fry for 8 to 10 minutes more until the internal temperature reaches 75ºC and the insides are no longer pink. Let sit for 5 minutes before serving.

Crispy Chicken Cordon Bleu

Prep time: 15 minutes | Cook time: 13 to 15 minutes | Serves 4

4 chicken breast fillets
35 g chopped ham
25 g grated Swiss or Gruyère cheese
30 g flour
Pinch salt

Freshly ground black pepper, to taste
½ tsp. dried marjoram
1 egg
120 g panko bread crumbs
Olive oil for misting

1. Preheat the air fryer to 190ºC.
2. Put the chicken breast fillets on a work surface and gently press them with the palm of your hand to make them a bit thinner. Don't tear the meat.
3. In a small bowl, combine the ham and cheese. Divide this mixture among the chicken fillets. Wrap the

chicken around the filling to enclose it, using toothpicks to hold the chicken together.

4. In a shallow bowl, mix the flour, salt, pepper, and marjoram. In another bowl, beat the egg. Spread the bread crumbs out on a plate.
5. Dip the chicken into the flour mixture, then into the egg, then into the bread crumbs to coat thoroughly.
6. Put the chicken in the air fryer basket and mist with olive oil.
7. Bake for 13 to 15 minutes or until the chicken is thoroughly cooked to 75ºC. Carefully remove the toothpicks and serve.

Chicken Burgers with Ham and Cheese

Prep time: 12 minutes | Cook time: 13 to 16 minutes | Serves 4

35 g soft bread crumbs
3 tbsps. milk
1 egg, beaten
½ tsp. dried thyme
Pinch salt

Freshly ground black pepper, to taste
567 g chicken mince
40 g finely chopped ham
25 g grated Havarti cheese
Olive oil for misting

1. Preheat the air fryer to 180ºC.
2. In a medium bowl, combine the bread crumbs, milk, egg, thyme, salt, and pepper. Add the chicken and mix gently but thoroughly with clean hands.
3. Form the chicken into eight thin patties and place on waxed paper.
4. Top four of the patties with the ham and cheese. Top with remaining four patties and gently press the edges together to seal, so the ham and cheese mixture is in the middle of the burger.
5. Place the burgers in the basket and mist with olive oil. Bake for 13 to 16 minutes or until the chicken is thoroughly cooked to 75ºC as measured with a meat thermometer. Serve immediately.

Chicken and Vegetable Fajitas

Prep time: 15 minutes | Cook time: 23 minutes | Serves 6

Chicken:
454 g boneless, skinless chicken thighs, cut crosswise into thirds
1 tbsp. vegetable oil
4½ tsps. taco seasoning
Vegetables
60 g sliced onion
100 g sliced pepper
1 or 2 jalapeños, quartered lengthwise

1 tbsp. vegetable oil
½ tsp. salt
½ tsp. ground cumin
For Serving:
Tortillas
Sour cream
Shredded cheese
Guacamole
Salsa

1. Preheat the air fryer to 190ºC.
2. For the chicken: In a medium bowl, toss together the chicken, vegetable oil, and taco seasoning to coat.
3. For the vegetables: In a separate bowl, toss together the onion, pepper, jalapeño (s), vegetable oil, salt, and cumin to coat.
4. Place the chicken in the air fryer basket. Air fry for 10 minutes. Add the vegetables to the basket, toss everything together to blend the seasonings, and air fry for 13 minutes more. Use a meat thermometer to ensure the chicken has reached an internal temperature of 75ºC.
5. Transfer the chicken and vegetables to a serving platter. Serve with tortillas and the desired fajita fixings.

Coconut Chicken Meatballs

Prep time: 10 minutes | Cook time: 14 minutes | Serves 4

454 g chicken mince
2 spring onions, finely chopped
40 g chopped fresh coriander leaves
20 g unsweetened shredded coconut
1 tbsp. hoisin sauce

1 tbsp. soy sauce
2 tsps. sriracha or other hot sauce
1 tsp. toasted sesame oil
½ tsp. salt
1 tsp. black pepper

1. Preheat the air fryer to 180ºC.
2. In a large bowl, gently mix the chicken, spring onions, coriander, coconut, hoisin, soy sauce, sriracha, sesame oil, salt, and pepper until thoroughly combined (the mixture will be wet and sticky).
3. Place a sheet of parchment paper in the air fryer basket. Using a small scoop or teaspoon, drop rounds of the mixture in a single layer onto the parchment paper.
4. Air fry for 10 minutes, turning the meatballs halfway through the cooking time. Increase the temperature to 200ºC and air fry for 4 minutes more to brown the outsides of the meatballs. Use a meat thermometer to ensure the meatballs have reached an internal temperature of 75ºC.
5. Transfer the meatballs to a serving platter. Repeat with any remaining chicken mixture. Serve.

Turkish Chicken Kebabs

Prep time: 15 minutes | Cook time: 15 minutes | Serves 4

70 g plain Greek yogurt
1 tbsp. minced garlic
1 tbsp. tomato paste
1 tbsp. fresh lemon juice
1 tbsp. vegetable oil
1 tsp. salt
1 tsp. ground cumin

1 tsp. sweet Hungarian paprika
½ tsp. ground cinnamon
½ tsp. black pepper
½ tsp. cayenne pepper
454 g boneless, skinless chicken thighs, quartered crosswise

1. In a large bowl, combine the yogurt, garlic, tomato paste, lemon juice, vegetable oil, salt, cumin, paprika, cinnamon, black pepper, and cayenne. Stir until the spices are blended into the yogurt.
2. Add the chicken to the bowl and toss until well coated. Marinate at room temperature for 30 minutes, or cover and refrigerate for up to 24 hours.
3. Preheat the air fryer to 190ºC.
4. Arrange the chicken in a single layer in the air fryer basket. Air fry for 10 minutes. Turn the chicken and air fry for 5 minutes more. Use a meat thermometer to ensure the chicken has reached an internal temperature of 75ºC.
5. Serve warm.

Chapter 5 Fish and Seafood

Oyster Po'Boy

Prep time: 20 minutes | Cook time: 5 minutes | Serves 4

100 g plain flour
40 g yellow cornmeal
1 tbsp. Cajun seasoning
1 tsp. salt
2 large eggs, beaten
1 tsp. hot sauce
454 g pre-shucked oysters
1 (24-cm) French baguette, quartered and sliced horizontally
Tartar Sauce, as needed
45 g shredded lettuce, divided
2 tomatoes, cut into slices
Cooking spray

1. In a shallow bowl, whisk the flour, cornmeal, Cajun seasoning, and salt until blended. In a second shallow bowl, whisk together the eggs and hot sauce.
2. One at a time, dip the oysters in the cornmeal mixture, the eggs, and again in the cornmeal, coating thoroughly.
3. Preheat the air fryer to 200ºC. Line the air fryer basket with parchment paper.
4. Place the oysters on the parchment and spritz with oil.
5. Air fry for 2 minutes. Shake the basket, spritz the oysters with oil, and air fry for 3 minutes more until lightly browned and crispy.
6. Spread each sandwich half with Tartar Sauce. Assemble the po'boys by layering each sandwich with fried oysters, 20 g shredded lettuce, and 2 tomato slices.
7. Serve immediately.

Crab Cakes with Sriracha Mayonnaise

Prep time: 15 minutes | Cook time: 10 minutes | Serves 4

Sriracha Mayonnaise:
240 g mayonnaise
1 tbsp. sriracha
1½ tsps. freshly squeezed lemon juice
Crab Cakes:
1 tsp. extra-virgin olive oil
30 g finely diced red pepper
20 g diced onion
25 g diced celery
454 g lump crab meat
1 tsp. Old Bay seasoning
1 egg
1½ tsps. freshly squeezed lemon juice
220 g panko bread crumbs, divided
Vegetable oil, for spraying

1. Mix the mayonnaise, sriracha, and lemon juice in a small bowl. Place ⅔ cup of the mixture in a separate bowl to form the base of the crab cakes. Cover the remaining sriracha mayonnaise and refrigerate. (This will become dipping sauce for the crab cakes once they are cooked.)

2. Heat the olive oil in a heavy-bottomed, medium skillet over medium-high heat. Add the pepper, onion, and celery and sauté for 3 minutes. Transfer the vegetables to the bowl with the reserved ⅔ cup of sriracha mayonnaise. Mix in the crab, Old Bay seasoning, egg, and lemon juice. Add 120 g of the panko. Form the crab mixture into 8 cakes. Dredge the cakes in the remaining ¾ cup of panko, turning to coat. Place on a baking sheet. Cover and refrigerate for at least 1 hour and up to 8 hours.

3. Preheat the air fryer to 190ºC. Spray the air fryer basket with oil. Working in batches as needed so as not to overcrowd the basket, place the chilled crab cakes in a single layer in the basket. Spray the crab cakes with oil. Bake until golden brown, 8 to 10 minutes, carefully turning halfway through cooking. Remove to a platter and keep warm. Repeat with the remaining crab cakes as needed. Serve the crab cakes immediately with sriracha mayonnaise dipping sauce.

Baja Fish Tacos

Prep time: 15 minutes | Cook time: 10 minutes | Serves 4

Fried Fish:
454 g tilapia fillets (or other mild white fish)
66 g plain flour
1 tsp. garlic powder
1 tsp. salt
¼ tsp. cayenne pepper
122 g mayonnaise
3 tbsps. milk
220 g panko bread crumbs
Vegetable oil, for spraying

Tacos:
8 corn tortillas
¼ head red or green cabbage, shredded
1 ripe avocado, halved and each half cut into 4 slices
340 g pico de gallo or other fresh salsa
Dollop of Mexican crema
1 lime, cut into wedges

1. To make the fish, cut the fish fillets into strips 6 to 8-cm long and 2-cm wide. Combine the flour, garlic powder, salt, and cayenne pepper on a plate and whisk to combine. In a shallow bowl, whisk the mayonnaise and milk together. Place the panko on a separate plate. Dredge the fish strips in the seasoned flour, shaking off any excess. Dip the strips in the mayonnaise mixture, coating them completely, then dredge in the panko, shaking off any excess. Place the fish strips on a plate or rack.

2. Preheat the air fryer to 200ºC. Working in batches, spray half the fish strips with oil and arrange them in the air fryer basket, taking care not to crowd them. Air fry for 4 minutes, then flip and air fry for another 3 to 4 minutes until the outside is brown and crisp and the inside is opaque and flakes easily with a fork. Repeat with the remaining strips.

3. Heat the tortillas in the microwave or on the stovetop. To assemble the tacos, place 2 fish strips inside each tortilla. Top with shredded cabbage, a slice of avocado, pico de gallo, and a dollop of crema. Serve with a lime wedge on the side.

Salmon Patties

Prep time: 10 minutes | Cook time: 8 minutes | Serves 4

2 (142 g) cans salmon, flaked
2 large eggs, beaten
10 gminced onion
75 g panko bread crumbs
1½ tsps. Italian-Style seasoning
1 tsp. garlic powder
Cooking spray

1. In a medium bowl, stir together the salmon, eggs, and onion.
2. In a small bowl, whisk the bread crumbs, Italian-Style seasoning, and garlic powder until blended. Add the bread crumb mixture to the salmon mixture and stir until blended. Shape the mixture into 8 patties.
3. Preheat the air fryer to 180ºC. Line the air fryer basket with parchment paper.
4. Working in batches as needed, place the patties on the parchment and spritz with oil.
5. Bake for 4 minutes. Flip, spritz the patties with oil, and bake for 4 to 8 minutes more, until browned and firm. Serve.

Prawn Dejonghe Skewers

Prep time: 10 minutes | Cook time: 15 minutes | Serves 4

2 tsps. sherry
3 tbsps. unsalted butter, melted
126 g panko bread crumbs
3 cloves garlic, minced
17 g minced flat-leaf parsley, plus more for garnish
1 tsp. salt
Pinch of cayenne pepper
680 g prawn, peeled and deveined
Vegetable oil, for spraying
Lemon wedges, for serving

1. Stir the sherry and melted butter together in a shallow bowl or pie plate and whisk until combined. Set aside. Whisk together the panko, garlic, parsley, salt, and cayenne pepper on a large plate or shallow bowl.
2. Thread the prawns onto metal skewers designed for the air fryer or bamboo skewers, 3 to 4 per skewer. Dip 1 prawn skewer in the butter mixture, then dredge in the panko mixture until each prawn is lightly coated. Place the skewer on a plate or rimmed baking sheet and repeat the process with the remaining skewers.
3. Preheat the air fryer to 180ºC. Arrange 4 skewers in the air fryer basket. Spray the skewers with oil and air fry for 8 minutes, until the bread crumbs are golden brown and the prawns are cooked through. Transfer the cooked skewers to a serving plate and keep warm while cooking the remaining 4 skewers in the air fryer.
4. Sprinkle the cooked skewers with additional fresh parsley and serve with lemon wedges if desired.

Jalea

Prep time: 20 minutes | Cook time: 10 minutes | Serves 4

Salsa Criolla:
½ red onion, thinly sliced
2 tomatoes, diced
1 serrano or jalapeño pepper, deseeded and diced
1 clove garlic, minced
15 g chopped fresh coriander
Pinch of salt
3 limes

Fried Seafood:
454 g firm, white-fleshed fish such as cod (add an extra 227-g fish if not using prawn)
20 large or jumbo prawn, shelled and deveined
35 g plain flour
30 g cornflour
1 tsp. garlic powder
1 tsp. salt
¼ tsp. cayenne pepper
252 g panko bread crumbs
2 eggs, beaten with 2 tbsps. water
Vegetable oil, for spraying
Mayonnaise or tartar sauce, for serving (optional)

1. To make the Salsa Criolla, combine the red onion, tomatoes, pepper, garlic, coriander, and salt in a medium bowl. Add the juice and zest of 2 of the limes. Refrigerate the salad while you make the fish.
2. To make the seafood, cut the fish fillets into strips approximately 4-cm long and 2-cm wide. Place the flour, cornflour, garlic powder, salt, and cayenne pepper on a plate and whisk to combine. Place the panko on a separate plate. Dredge the fish strips in the seasoned flour mixture, shaking off any excess. Dip the strips in the egg mixture, coating them completely, then dredge in the panko, shaking off any excess. Place the fish strips on a plate or rack. Repeat with the prawn, if using.
3. Spray the air fryer basket with oil, and preheat the air fryer to 200ºC. Working in 2 or 3 batches, arrange the fish and prawn in a single layer in the basket, taking care not to crowd the basket. Spray with oil. Air fry for 5 minutes, then flip and air fry for another 4 to 5 minutes until the outside is brown and crisp and the inside of the fish is opaque and flakes easily with a fork. Repeat with the remaining seafood.
4. Place the fried seafood on a platter. Use a slotted spoon to remove the salsa criolla from the bowl, leaving behind any liquid that has accumulated. Place the salsa criolla on top of the fried seafood. Serve immediately with the remaining lime, cut into wedges, and mayonnaise or tartar sauce as desired.

Cajun Fish Fillets

Prep time: 15 minutes | Cook time: 6 minutes | Serves 4

100 g plain flour
40 g yellow cornmeal
1 large egg, beaten

58 g Cajun seasoning
4 (113-g) catfish fillets
Cooking spray

1. In a shallow bowl, whisk the flour and cornmeal until blended. Place the egg in a second shallow bowl and the Cajun seasoning in a third shallow bowl.
2. One at a time, dip the catfish fillets in the breading, the egg, and the Cajun seasoning, coating thoroughly.
3. Preheat the air fryer to 150ºC. Line the air fryer basket with parchment paper.
4. Place the coated fish on the parchment and spritz with oil.
5. Bake for 3 minutes. Flip the fish, spritz it with oil, and bake for 3 to 5 minutes more until the fish flakes easily with a fork and reaches an internal temperature of 65ºC. Serve warm.

Blackened Fish

Prep time: 15 minutes | Cook time: 8 minutes | Serves 4

1 large egg, beaten
Blackened seasoning, as needed
2 tbsps. light brown sugar

4 (113- g) tilapia fillets
Cooking spray

1. In a shallow bowl, place the beaten egg. In a second shallow bowl, stir together the Blackened seasoning and the brown sugar.
2. One at a time, dip the fish fillets in the egg, then the brown sugar mixture, coating thoroughly.
3. Preheat the air fryer to 150ºC. Line the air fryer basket with parchment paper.
4. Place the coated fish on the parchment and spritz with oil.
5. Bake for 4 minutes. Flip the fish, spritz it with oil, and bake for 4 to 6 minutes more until the fish is white inside and flakes easily with a fork.
6. Serve immediately.

Fried Catfish with Dijon Sauce

Prep time: 20 minutes | Cook time: 7 minutes | Serves 4

4 tbsps. butter, melted
2 tsps. Worcestershire sauce, divided
1 tsp. lemon pepper
126 g panko bread crumbs

4 (113-g) catfish fillets
Cooking spray
130 g sour cream
1 tbsp. Dijon mustard

1. In a shallow bowl, stir together the melted butter, 1 tsp. of Worcestershire sauce, and the lemon pepper. Place the bread crumbs in another shallow bowl.
2. One at a time, dip both sides of the fillets in the butter mixture, then the bread crumbs, coating thoroughly.
3. Preheat the air fryer to 150ºC. Line the air fryer basket with parchment paper.
4. Place the coated fish on the parchment and spritz with oil.
5. Bake for 4 minutes. Flip the fish, spritz it with oil, and bake for 3 to 6 minutes more, depending on the thickness of the fillets, until the fish flakes easily with a fork.
6. In a small bowl, stir together the sour cream, Dijon, and remaining 1 tsp. of Worcestershire sauce. This sauce can be made 1 day in advance and refrigerated before serving. Serve with the fried fish.

Trout Amandine with Lemon Butter Sauce

Prep time: 20 minutes | Cook time:8 minutes | Serves 4

Trout Amandine:
90 g toasted almonds
30 g grated Parmesan cheese
1 tsp. salt
½ tsp. freshly ground black pepper
2 tbsps. butter, melted
4 (113-g) trout fillets, or salmon fillets
Cooking spray

Lemon Butter Sauce:
8 tbsps. butter, melted
2 tbsps. freshly squeezed lemon juice
½ tsp. Worcestershire sauce
½ tsp. salt
½ tsp. freshly ground black pepper
¼ tsp. hot sauce

1. In a blender or food processor, pulse the almonds for 5 to 10 seconds until finely processed. Transfer to a shallow bowl and whisk in the Parmesan cheese, salt, and pepper. Place the melted butter in another shallow bowl.
2. One at a time, dip the fish in the melted butter, then the almond mixture, coating thoroughly.
3. Preheat the air fryer to 150ºC. Line the air fryer basket with parchment paper.
4. Place the coated fish on the parchment and spritz with oil.
5. Bake for 4 minutes. Flip the fish, spritz it with oil, and bake for 4 minutes more until the fish flakes easily with a fork.
6. In a small bowl, whisk the butter, lemon juice, Worcestershire sauce, salt, pepper, and hot sauce until blended.
7. Serve with the fish.

Tuna-Stuffed Quinoa Patties

Prep time: 10 minutes | Cook time: 15 minutes | Serves 4

340 g quinoa
4 slices white bread with crusts removed
120 ml milk
3 eggs
283 g tuna packed in olive oil, drained

2 to 3 lemons
Salt and pepper, to taste
157 g panko bread crumbs
Vegetable oil, for spraying
Lemon wedges, for serving

1. Rinse the quinoa in a fine-mesh sieve until the water runs clear. Bring 960 ml of salted water to a boil. Add the quinoa, cover, and reduce heat to low. Simmer the quinoa covered until most of the water is absorbed and the quinoa is tender, 15 to 20 minutes. Drain and allow to cool to room temperature. Meanwhile, soak the bread in the milk.
2. Mix the drained quinoa with the soaked bread and 2 of the eggs in a large bowl and mix thoroughly. In a medium bowl, combine the tuna, the remaining egg, and the juice and zest of 1 of the lemons. Season well with salt and pepper. Spread the panko on a plate.
3. Scoop up approximately 95 g of the quinoa mixture and flatten into a patty. Place a heaping tbsp. of the tuna mixture in the centre of the patty and close the quinoa around the tuna. Flatten the patty slightly to create an oval-shaped croquette. Dredge both sides of the croquette in the panko. Repeat with the remaining quinoa and tuna.
4. Spray the air fryer basket with oil to prevent sticking, and preheat the air fryer to 200ºC. Arrange 4 or 5 of the croquettes in the basket, taking care to avoid overcrowding. Spray the tops of the croquettes with oil. Air fry for 8 minutes until the top side is browned and crispy. Carefully turn the croquettes over and spray the second side with oil. Air fry until the second side is browned and crispy, another 7 minutes. Repeat with the remaining croquettes.
5. Serve the croquetas warm with plenty of lemon wedges for spritzing.

Fried Prawn

Prep time: 15 minutes | Cook time: 5 minutes | Serves 4

66 g self-rising flour
1 tsp. paprika
1 tsp. salt
½ tsp. freshly ground black pepper
1 large egg, beaten

126 g finely crushed panko bread crumbs
20 frozen large prawn (about 907-g), peeled and
deveined
Cooking spray

1. In a shallow bowl, whisk the flour, paprika, salt, and pepper until blended. Add the beaten egg to a second shallow bowl and the bread crumbs to a third.
2. One at a time, dip the prawns into the flour, the egg, and the bread crumbs, coating thoroughly.
3. Preheat the air fryer to 200ºC. Line the air fryer basket with parchment paper.
4. Place the prawns on the parchment and spritz with oil.
5. Air fry for 2 minutes. Shake the basket, spritz the prawns with oil, and air fry for 3 minutes more until lightly browned and crispy. Serve hot.

Traditional Tuna Melt

Prep time: 10 minutes | Cook time: 12 minutes | Serves 2

2 cans unsalted albacore tuna, drained
122 g mayonnaise
½ tsp. salt
¼ tsp. ground black pepper
4 slices sourdough bread

4 pieces sliced Cheddar cheese
2 tbsps. crispy fried onions
Cooking spray
¼ tsp. granulated garlic

1. Preheat the air fryer to 200ºC.
2. In a medium bowl, combine the tuna, mayonnaise, salt, and pepper, and mix well. Set aside.
3. Assemble the sandwiches by laying out the bread and then adding 1 slice of cheese on top of each piece.
4. Sprinkle the fried onions on top of the cheese on 2 of the slices of bread.
5. Divide the tuna between the 2 slices of bread with the onions.
6. Take the remaining 2 slices of bread that have only cheese on them, and place them cheese-side down on top of the tuna.
7. Place one sandwich in the air fryer basket, spray with cooking spray, and air fry for 6 minutes.
8. Using a spatula, flip the sandwich over, spray it again, and air fry for another 6 minutes, or until golden brown. Sprinkle with the garlic immediately after removing from the air fryer basket. Repeat with the other sandwich.
9. Allow the sandwiches to sit for 1 to 2 minutes before cutting and serving.
10. Serve immediately.

New Orleans-Style Crab Cakes

Prep time: 10 minutes | Cook time: 8 to 10 minutes | Serves 4

160 g bread crumbs
2 tsps. Creole Seasoning
1 tsp. dry mustard
1 tsp. salt
1 tsp. freshly ground black pepper
220 g cups crab meat

2 large eggs, beaten
1 tsp. butter, melted
25 g minced onion
Cooking spray
Pecan Tartar Sauce, for serving

1. Preheat the air fryer to 180ºC. Line the air fryer basket with parchment paper.
2. In a medium bowl, whisk the bread crumbs, Creole Seasoning, dry mustard, salt, and pepper until blended. Add the crab meat, eggs, butter, and onion. Stir until blended. Shape the crab mixture into 8 patties.
3. Place the crab cakes on the parchment and spritz with oil.
4. Air fry for 4 minutes. Flip the cakes, spritz them with oil, and air fry for 4 to 6 minutes more until the outsides are firm and a fork inserted into the centre comes out clean. Serve with the Pecan Tartar Sauce.

Chapter 6 Meats

Air Fried Lamb Ribs

Prep time: 5 minutes | Cook time: 18 minutes | Serves 4

2 tbsps. mustard
454 g lamb ribs
1 tsp. rosemary, chopped
Salt and ground black pepper, to taste
15 g mint leaves, chopped
280 g Greek yogurt

1. Preheat the air fryer to 180ºC.
2. Use a brush to apply the mustard to the lamb ribs, and season with rosemary, salt, and pepper.
3. Air fry the ribs in the air fryer for 18 minutes.
4. Meanwhile, combine the mint leaves and yogurt in a bowl.
5. Remove the lamb ribs from the air fryer when cooked and serve with the mint yogurt.

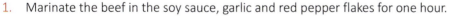

Mongolian Flank Steak

Prep time: 20 minutes | Cook time: 15 minutes | Serves 4

680 g flank steak, thinly sliced on the bias into ½ cm strips
Marinade:
2 tbsps. soy sauce
1 clove garlic, smashed
Pinch crushed red pepper flakes
Sauce:
1 tbsp. vegetable oil
2 cloves garlic, minced
1 tbsp. finely grated fresh ginger
3 dried red chili peppers
180 ml soy sauce
180 ml chicken stock
5 to 6 tbsps. brown sugar
60 g cornflour, divided
1 bunch spring onions, sliced into 4-cm pieces

1. Marinate the beef in the soy sauce, garlic and red pepper flakes for one hour.
2. In the meantime, make the sauce. Preheat a small saucepan over medium heat on the stovetop. Add the oil, garlic, ginger and dried chili peppers and sauté for just a minute or two. Add the soy sauce, chicken stock and brown sugar and continue to simmer for a few minutes. Dissolve 3 tbsps. of cornflour in 3 tbsps. of water and stir this into the saucepan. Stir the sauce over medium heat until it thickens. Set this aside.
3. Preheat the air fryer to 200ºC.
4. Remove the beef from the marinade and transfer it to a zipper sealable plastic bag with the remaining cornflour. Shake it around to completely coat the beef and transfer the coated strips of beef to a baking sheet or plate, shaking off any excess cornflour. Spray the strips with vegetable oil on all sides and transfer them to the air fryer basket.
5. Air fry for 15 minutes, shaking the basket to toss and rotate the beef strips throughout the cooking process. Add the spring onions for the last 4 minutes of the cooking. Transfer the hot beef strips and spring onions to a bowl and toss with the sauce, coating all the beef strips with the sauce. Serve warm.

Cheesy Beef Meatballs

Prep time: 5 minutes | Cook time: 18 minutes | Serves 6

454 g beef mince
45 g grated Parmesan cheese
1 tbsp. minced garlic
110 g Mozzarella cheese
1 tsp. freshly ground pepper

1. Preheat the air fryer to 200ºC.
2. In a bowl, mix all the ingredients together.
3. Roll the meat mixture into 5 generous meatballs.
4. Air fry inside the air fryer at 74ºC for about 18 minutes.
5. Serve immediately.

Lamb Burger

Prep time: 15 minutes | Cook time: 16 minutes | Serves 3 to 4

2 tsps. olive oil
⅓ onion, finely chopped
1 clove garlic, minced
454 g lamb mince
2 tbsps. fresh parsley, finely chopped
1½ tsps. fresh oregano, finely chopped
90 g black olives, finely chopped
60 g crumbled feta cheese
½ tsp. salt
freshly ground black pepper
4 thick pita breads
toppings and condiments

1. Preheat a medium skillet over medium-high heat on the stovetop. Add the olive oil and cook the onion until tender, but not browned about 4 to 5 minutes. Add the garlic and cook for another minute. Transfer the onion and garlic to a mixing bowl and add the ground lamb, parsley, oregano, olives, feta cheese, salt and pepper. Gently mix the ingredients together.
2. Divide the mixture into 3 or 4 equal portions and then form the hamburgers, being careful not to over-handle the meat. One good way to do this is to throw the meat back and forth between the hands like a baseball, packing the meat each time you catch it. Flatten the balls into patties, making an indentation in the centre of each patty. Flatten the sides of the patties as well to make it easier to fit them into the air fryer basket.
3. Preheat the air fryer to 190ºC.
4. If you don't have room for all four burgers, air fry two or three burgers at a time for 8 minutes. Flip the burgers over and air fry for another 8 minutes. If you cooked the burgers in batches, return the first batch of burgers to the air fryer for the last two minutes of cooking to re-heat. This should give you a medium-well burger. If you'd prefer a medium-rare burger, shorten the cooking time to about 13 minutes. Remove the burgers to a resting plate and let the burgers rest for a few minutes before dressing and serving.
5. While the burgers are resting, bake the pita breads in the air fryer for 2 minutes. Tuck the burgers into the toasted pita breads, or wrap the pitas around the burgers and serve with a tzatziki sauce or some mayonnaise.

Citrus Pork Loin Roast

Prep time: 10 minutes | Cook time: 45 minutes | Serves 8

1 tbsp. lime juice
1 tbsp. orange marmalade
1 tsp. coarse brown mustard
1 tsp. curry powder
1 tsp. dried lemongrass
907 g boneless pork loin roast
Salt and ground black pepper, to taste
Cooking spray

1. Preheat the air fryer to 180ºC.
2. Mix the lime juice, marmalade, mustard, curry powder, and lemongrass.
3. Rub mixture all over the surface of the pork loin. Season with salt and pepper.
4. Spray air fryer basket with cooking spray and place pork roast diagonally in the basket.
5. Air fry for approximately 45 minutes, until the internal temperature reaches at least 65ºC.
6. Wrap roast in foil and let rest for 10 minutes before slicing.
7. Serve immediately.

Lollipop Lamb Chops

Prep time: 15 minutes | Cook time: 7 minutes | Serves 4

½ small clove garlic
15 g packed fresh parsley
50 g packed fresh mint
½ tsp. lemon juice
22 g grated Parmesan cheese
50 g shelled pistachios
¼ tsp. salt
120 ml olive oil
8 lamb chops (1 rack)
2 tbsps. vegetable oil
Salt and freshly ground black pepper, to taste
1 tbsp. dried rosemary, chopped
1 tbsp. dried thyme

1. Make the pesto by combining the garlic, parsley and mint in a food processor and process until finely chopped. Add the lemon juice, Parmesan cheese, pistachios and salt. Process until all the ingredients have turned into a paste. With the processor running, slowly pour the olive oil in. Scrape the sides of the processor with a spatula and process for another 30 seconds.
2. Preheat the air fryer to 200ºC.
3. Rub both sides of the lamb chops with vegetable oil and season with salt, pepper, rosemary and thyme, pressing the herbs into the meat gently with the fingers. Transfer the lamb chops to the air fryer basket.
4. Air fry the lamb chops for 5 minutes. Flip the chops over and air fry for an additional 2 minutes.
5. Serve the lamb chops with mint pesto drizzled on top.

Pepperoni and Pepper Pockets

Prep time: 5 minutes | Cook time: 8 minutes | Serves 4

4 bread slices, 2-cm thick
Olive oil, for misting
24 slices pepperoni

28 g roasted red peppers, drained and patted dry
28 g Pepper Jack cheese, cut into 4 slices

1. Preheat the air fryer to 180ºC.
2. Spray both sides of bread slices with olive oil.
3. Stand slices upright and cut a deep slit in the top to create a pocket (almost to the bottom crust, but not all the way through).
4. Stuff each bread pocket with 6 slices of pepperoni, a large strip of roasted red pepper, and a slice of cheese.
5. Put bread pockets in air fryer basket, standing up. Air fry for 8 minutes, until filling is heated through and bread is lightly browned.
6. Serve hot.

Pork and Pinto Bean Gorditas

Prep time: 20 minutes | Cook time: 21 minutes | Serves 4

454 g lean pork mince
2 tbsps. chili powder
2 tbsps. ground cumin
1 tsp. dried oregano
2 tsps. paprika
1 tsp. garlic powder
120 ml water
1 (425-g) can pinto beans, drained and rinsed
117 g taco sauce
Salt and freshly ground black pepper, to taste

470 g grated Cheddar cheese
5 (24-cm) flour tortillas
4 (16-cm) crispy corn tortilla shells
60 g shredded lettuce
1 tomato, diced
60 g sliced black olives
Sour cream, for serving
Tomato salsa, for serving
Cooking spray

1. Preheat the air fryer to 200ºC. Spritz the air fryer basket with cooking spray.
2. Put the pork mince in the air fryer basket and air fry at 200ºC for 10 minutes, stirring a few times to gently break up the meat. Combine the chili powder, cumin, oregano, paprika, garlic powder and water in a small bowl. Stir the spice mixture into the browned pork. Stir in the beans and taco sauce and air fry for an additional minute. Transfer the pork mixture to a bowl. Season with salt and freshly ground black pepper.
3. Sprinkle 40 g of the grated cheese in the centre of the flour tortillas, leaving a 4-cm border around the edge free of cheese and filling. Divide the pork mixture among the four tortillas, placing it on top of the cheese. Put a crunchy corn tortilla on top of the pork and top with shredded lettuce, diced tomatoes, and black olives. Cut the remaining flour tortilla into 4 quarters. These quarters of tortilla will serve as the bottom of the gordita. Put one quarter tortilla on top of each gordita and fold the edges of the bottom flour tortilla up over the sides, enclosing the filling. While holding the seams down, brush the bottom of the gordita with olive oil and place the seam side down on the countertop while you finish the remaining three gorditas.
4. Preheat the air fryer to 190ºC.
5. Air fry one gordita at a time. Transfer the gordita carefully to the air fryer basket, seam side down. Brush or spray the top tortilla with oil and air fry for 5 minutes. Carefully turn the gordita over and air fry for an additional 4 to 5 minutes until both sides are browned. When finished air frying all four gorditas, layer them back into the air fryer for an additional minute to make sure they are all warm before serving with sour cream and salsa.

Orange Pork Tenderloin

Prep time: 15 minutes | Cook time: 23 minutes | Serves 3 to 4

2 tbsps. brown sugar
2 tsps. cornflour
2 tsps. Dijon mustard
120 ml orange juice
½ tsp. soy sauce
2 tsps. grated fresh ginger

60 ml white wine
Zest of 1 orange
454 g pork tenderloin
Salt and freshly ground black pepper, to taste
Oranges, halved, for garnish
Fresh parsley, for garnish

1. Combine the brown sugar, cornflour, Dijon mustard, orange juice, soy sauce, ginger, white wine and orange zest in a small saucepan and bring the mixture to a boil on the stovetop. Lower the heat and simmer while you air fry the pork tenderloin or until the sauce has thickened.
2. Preheat the air fryer to 190ºC.
3. Season all sides of the pork tenderloin with salt and freshly ground black pepper. Transfer the tenderloin to the air fryer basket.
4. Air fry for 20 to 23 minutes, or until the internal temperature reaches 65ºC. Flip the tenderloin over halfway through the cooking process and baste with the sauce.
5. Transfer the tenderloin to a cutting board and let it rest for 5 minutes. Slice the pork at a slight angle and serve immediately with orange halves and fresh parsley.
6. Serve immediately.

Lamb Meatballs

Prep time: 20 minutes | Cook time: 8 minutes | Serves 4

Meatballs:
½ small onion, finely diced
1 clove garlic, minced
454 g lamb mince
2 tbsps. fresh parsley, finely chopped (plus more for garnish)
2 tsps. fresh oregano, finely chopped
2 tbsps. milk
1 egg yolk
Salt and freshly ground black pepper, to taste

80 g crumbled feta cheese, for garnish
Tomato Sauce:
2 tbsps. butter
1 clove garlic, smashed
Pinch crushed red pepper flakes
¼ tsp. ground cinnamon
1 (794-g) can crushed tomatoes
Salt, to taste
Olive oil, for greasing

1. Combine all ingredients for the meatballs in a large bowl and mix just until everything is combined. Shape the mixture into 3-cm balls or shape the meat between two spoons to make quenelles.
2. Preheat the air fryer to 200ºC.
3. While the air fryer is preheating, start the quick tomato sauce. Put the butter, garlic and red pepper flakes in a sauté pan and heat over medium heat on the stovetop. Let the garlic sizzle a little, but before the butter browns, add the cinnamon and tomatoes. Bring to a simmer and simmer for 15 minutes. Season with salt.
4. Grease the bottom of the air fryer basket with olive oil and transfer the meatballs to the air fryer basket in one layer, air frying in batches if necessary.
5. Air fry for 8 minutes, giving the basket a shake once during the cooking process to turn the meatballs over.
6. To serve, spoon a pool of the tomato sauce onto plates and add the meatballs. Sprinkle the feta cheese on top and garnish with more fresh parsley. Serve immediately.

Mushroom and Beef Meatloaf

Prep time: 10 minutes | Cook time: 25 minutes | Serves 4

454 g beef mince
1 egg, beaten
4 mushrooms, sliced
1 tbsp. thyme

1 small onion, chopped
3 tbsps. bread crumbs
Ground black pepper, to taste

1. Preheat the air fryer to 200ºC.
2. Put all the ingredients into a large bowl and combine entirely.
3. Transfer the meatloaf mixture into the loaf pan and move it to the air fryer basket.
4. Bake for 25 minutes. Slice up before serving.

Mozzarella Beef Brisket

Prep time: 5 minutes | Cook time: 25 minutes | Serves 6

340 g beef brisket
2 tsps. Italian herbs
2 tsps. butter

1 onion, sliced
198 g Mozzarella cheese, sliced

1. Preheat the air fryer to 185ºC.
2. Cut up the brisket into four equal slices and season with the Italian herbs.
3. Allow the butter to melt in the air fryer. Put the slices of beef inside along with the onion. Air fry for 25 minutes. Flip the brisket halfway through. Put a piece of Mozzarella on top of each piece of brisket in the last 5 minutes.
4. Serve immediately.

Potato and Prosciutto Salad

Prep time: 10 minutes | Cook time: 7 minutes | Serves 8

Salad:
1.8 kg potatoes, boiled and cubed
15 slices prosciutto, diced
166 g shredded Cheddar cheese
Dressing:

425 g sour cream
2 tbsps. mayonnaise
1 tsp. salt
1 tsp. black pepper
1 tsp. dried basil

1. Preheat the air fryer to 180ºC.
2. Put the potatoes, prosciutto, and Cheddar in a baking dish. Put it in the air fryer and air fry for 7 minutes.
3. In a separate bowl, mix the sour cream, mayonnaise, salt, pepper, and basil using a whisk.
4. Coat the salad with the dressing and serve.

Fast Lamb Satay

Prep time: 5 minutes | Cook time: 8 minutes | Serves 2

¼ tsp. cumin
1 tsp. ginger
½ tsps. nutmeg

Salt and ground black pepper, to taste
2 boneless lamb steaks
Cooking spray

1. Combine the cumin, ginger, nutmeg, salt and pepper in a bowl.
2. Cube the lamb steaks and massage the spice mixture into each one.
3. Leave to marinate for 10 minutes, then transfer onto metal skewers.
4. Preheat the air fryer to 200ºC.
5. Spritz the skewers with the cooking spray, then air fry them in the air fryer for 8 minutes.
6. Take care when removing them from the air fryer and serve.

Pork with Aloha Salsa

Prep time: 20 minutes | Cook time: 8 minutes | Serves 4

2 eggs
2 tbsps. milk
30 g flour
30 g panko bread crumbs
4 tsps. sesame seeds
454 g boneless, thin pork cutlets (1-cm thick)
Lemon pepper and salt, to taste
30 g cornflour
Cooking spray

Aloha Salsa:
225 g fresh pineapple, chopped in small pieces
15 g red onion, finely chopped
30 g green or red pepper, chopped
½ tsp. ground cinnamon
1 tsp. low-sodium soy sauce
⅛ tsp. crushed red pepper
⅛ tsp. ground black pepper

1. In a medium bowl, stir together all ingredients for salsa. Cover and refrigerate while cooking the pork.
2. Preheat the air fryer to 200ºC.
3. Beat the eggs and milk in a shallow dish.
4. In another shallow dish, mix the flour, panko, and sesame seeds.
5. Sprinkle pork cutlets with lemon pepper and salt.
6. Dip pork cutlets in cornflour, egg mixture, and then panko coating. Spray both sides with cooking spray.
7. Air fry the cutlets for 3 minutes. Turn cutlets over, spraying both sides, and continue air frying for 5 minutes or until well done.
8. Serve fried cutlets with salsa on the side.

Chapter 7 Wraps and Sandwiches

Nugget and Veggie Taco Wraps

Prep time: 5 minutes | Cook time: 15 minutes | Serves 4

1 tbsp. water
4 pieces commercial vegan nuggets, chopped
1 small yellow onion, diced
1 small red pepper, chopped
2 cobs grilled corn kernels
4 large corn tortillas
Mixed greens, for garnish

1. Preheat the air fryer to 200ºC.
2. Over a medium heat, sauté the nuggets in the water with the onion, corn kernels and pepper in a skillet, then remove from the heat.
3. Fill the tortillas with the nuggets and vegetables and fold them up. Transfer to the inside of the fryer and air fry for 15 minutes.
4. Once crispy, serve immediately, garnished with the mixed greens.

Lettuce Fajita Meatball Wraps

Prep time: 10 minutes | Cook time: 10 minutes | Serves 4

454 g 85% lean beef mince
130 g salsa, plus more for serving
15 g chopped onions
20 g diced green or red peppers
1 large egg, beaten
1 tsp. fine sea salt
½ tsp. chili powder
½ tsp. ground cumin
1 clove garlic, minced
Cooking spray
For Serving:
8 leaves Boston lettuce
Pico de gallo or salsa
Lime slices

1. Preheat the air fryer to 180ºC. Spray the air fryer basket with cooking spray.
2. In a large bowl, mix together all the ingredients until well combined.
3. Shape the meat mixture into eight 2-cm balls. Place the meatballs in the air fryer basket, leaving a little space between them. Air fry for 10 minutes, or until cooked through and no longer pink inside and the internal temperature reaches 63ºC.
4. Serve each meatball on a lettuce leaf, topped with pico de gallo or salsa. Serve with lime slices.

Tuna and Lettuce Wraps

Prep time: 10 minutes | Cook time: 4 to 7 minutes | Serves 4

454 g fresh tuna steak, cut into 2-cm cubes
1 tbsp. grated fresh ginger
2 garlic cloves, minced
½ tsp. toasted sesame oil
4 low-sodium whole-wheat tortillas
60 g low-fat mayonnaise
30 g shredded romaine lettuce
1 red pepper, thinly sliced

1. Preheat the air fryer to 200ºC.
2. In a medium bowl, mix the tuna, ginger, garlic, and sesame oil. Let it stand for 10 minutes.
3. Air fry the tuna in the air fryer basket for 4 to 7 minutes, or until lightly browned.
4. Make the wraps with the tuna, tortillas, mayonnaise, lettuce, and pepper.
5. Serve immediately.

Tuna Muffin Sandwich

Prep time: 8 minutes | Cook time: 4 to 8 minutes | Serves 4

1 (170-g) can chunk light tuna, drained
55 g mayonnaise
2 tbsps. mustard
1 tbsp. lemon juice
2 spring onions, minced
3 English muffins, split with a fork
3 tbsps. softened butter
6 thin slices Provolone or Muenster cheese

1. Preheat the air fryer to 200ºC.
2. In a small bowl, combine the tuna, mayonnaise, mustard, lemon juice, and spring onions. Set aside.
3. Butter the cut side of the English muffins. Bake, butter-side up, in the air fryer for 2 to 4 minutes, or until light golden brown. Remove the muffins from the air fryer basket.
4. Top each muffin with one slice of cheese and return to the air fryer. Bake for 2 to 4 minutes or until the cheese melts and starts to brown.
5. Remove the muffins from the air fryer, top with the tuna mixture, and serve.

Veggie Salsa Wraps

Prep time: 5 minutes | Cook time: 7 minutes | Serves 4

50 g red onion, sliced
1 courgette, chopped
1 poblano pepper, deseeded and finely chopped

1 head lettuce
130 g salsa
227 g Mozzarella cheese

1. Preheat the air fryer to 200ºC.
2. Place the red onion, courgette, and poblano pepper in the air fryer basket and air fry for 7 minutes, or until they are tender and fragrant.
3. Divide the veggie mixture among the lettuce leaves and spoon the salsa over the top. Finish off with Mozzarella cheese. Wrap the lettuce leaves around the filling.
4. Serve immediately.

Cheesy Prawn Sandwich

Prep time: 10 minutes | Cook time: 5 to 7 minutes | Serves 4

290 g shredded Colby, Cheddar, or Havarti cheese
1 (170-g) can tiny prawns, drained
3 tbsps. mayonnaise

2 tbsps. minced spring onion
4 slices whole grain or whole-wheat bread
2 tbsps. softened butter

1. Preheat the air fryer to 205ºC.
2. In a medium bowl, combine the cheese, prawn, mayonnaise, and spring onion, and mix well.
3. Spread this mixture on two of the slices of bread. Top with the other slices of bread to make two sandwiches. Spread the sandwiches lightly with butter.
4. Air fry for 5 to 7 minutes, or until the bread is browned and crisp and the cheese is melted.
5. Cut in half and serve warm.

Chicken Pita Sandwich

Prep time: 10 minutes | Cook time: 9 to 11 minutes | Serves 4

2 boneless, skinless chicken breasts, cut into 2-cm cubes
1 small red onion, sliced
1 red pepper, sliced
80 ml Italian salad dressing, divided

½ tsp. dried thyme
4 pita pockets, split
55 g torn butter lettuce
200 g chopped cherry tomatoes

1. Preheat the air fryer to 190ºC.
2. Place the chicken, onion, and pepper in the air fryer basket. Drizzle with 1 tbsp. of the Italian salad dressing, add the thyme, and toss.
3. Bake for 9 to 11 minutes, or until the chicken is 75ºC on a food thermometer, stirring once during cooking time.
4. Transfer the chicken and vegetables to a bowl and toss with the remaining salad dressing.
5. Assemble sandwiches with the pita pockets, butter lettuce, and cherry tomatoes. Serve immediately.

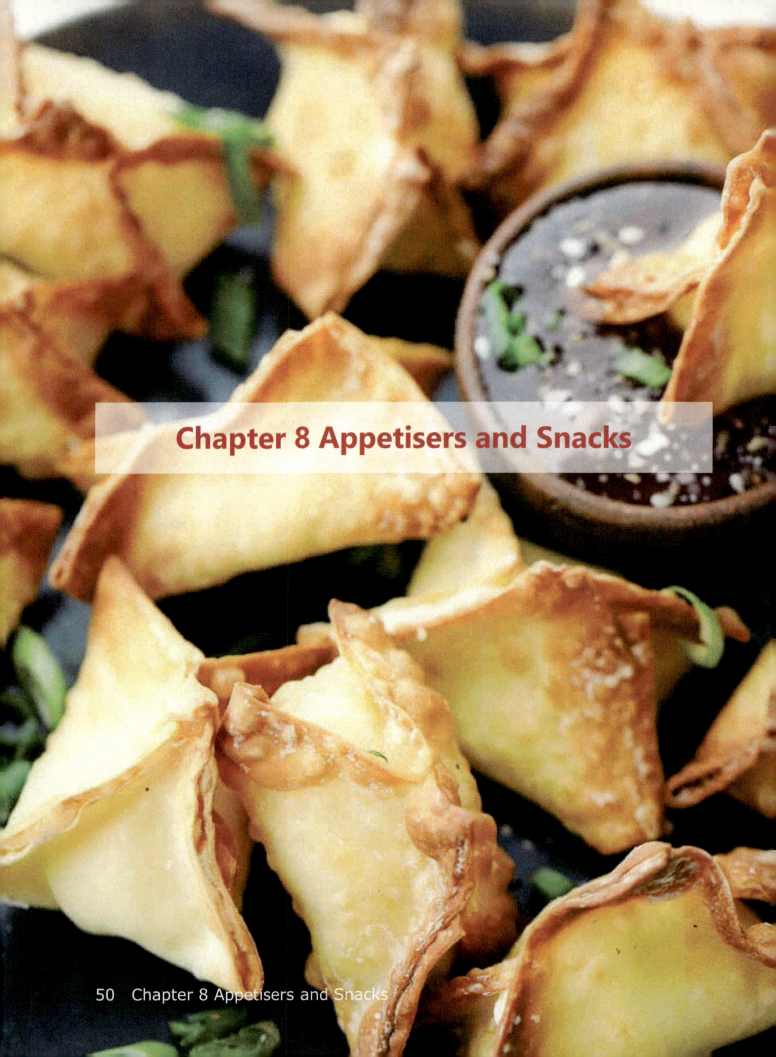

Chapter 8 Appetisers and Snacks

Air Fried Pot Stickers

Prep time: 10 minutes | Cook time: 18 to 20 minutes | Makes 30 pot stickers

25 g finely chopped cabbage
30 g finely chopped red pepper
2 spring onions, finely chopped
1 egg, beaten
2 tbsps. cocktail sauce
2 tsps. low-sodium soy sauce
30 wonton wrappers
1 tbsp. water, for brushing the wrappers

1. Preheat the air fryer to 180ºC.
2. In a small bowl, combine the cabbage, pepper, spring onions, egg, cocktail sauce, and soy sauce, and mix well.
3. Put about 1 tsp. of the mixture in the centre of each wonton wrapper. Fold the wrapper in half, covering the filling; dampen the edges with water, and seal. You can crimp the edges of the wrapper with your fingers so they look like the pot stickers you get in restaurants. Brush them with water.
4. Place the pot stickers in the air fryer basket and air fry in 2 batches for 9 to 10 minutes, or until the pot stickers are hot and the bottoms are lightly browned.
5. Serve hot.

Air Fried Spicy Olives

Prep time: 10 minutes | Cook time: 5 minutes | Serves 4

340 g pitted black extra-large olives
30 g plain flour
120 g panko bread crumbs
2 tsps. dried thyme
1 tsp. red pepper flakes
1 tsp. smoked paprika
1 egg beaten with 1 tbsp. water
Vegetable oil for spraying

1. Preheat the air fryer to 200ºC.
2. Drain the olives and place them on a paper towel–lined plate to dry.
3. Put the flour on a plate. Combine the panko, thyme, red pepper flakes, and paprika on a separate plate. Dip an olive in the flour, shaking off any excess, then coat with egg mixture. Dredge the olive in the panko mixture, pressing to make the crumbs adhere, and place the breaded olive on a platter. Repeat with the remaining olives.
4. Spray the olives with oil and place them in a single layer in the air fryer basket. Work in batches if necessary so as not to overcrowd the basket. Air fry for 5 minutes until the breading is browned and crispy. Serve warm.

Mozzarella Arancini

Prep time: 5 minutes | Cook time: 8 to 11 minutes | Makes 16 arancini

500 g cooked rice, cooled
2 eggs, beaten
180 g panko bread crumbs, divided
45 g grated Parmesan cheese
2 tbsps. minced fresh basil
16 1 ½ cm cubes Mozzarella cheese
2 tbsps. olive oil

1. Preheat the air fryer to 200ºC.
2. In a medium bowl, combine the rice, eggs, 60 g of the bread crumbs, Parmesan cheese, and basil. Form this mixture into 16 3-cm balls.
3. Poke a hole in each of the balls with your finger and insert a Mozzarella cube. Form the rice mixture firmly around the cheese.
4. On a shallow plate, combine the remaining 120 g of the bread crumbs with the olive oil and mix well. Roll the rice balls in the bread crumbs to coat.
5. Air fry the arancini in batches for 8 to 11 minutes or until golden brown.
6. Serve hot.

Cheesy Stuffed Mushrooms

Prep time: 10 minutes | Cook time: 8 to 12 minutes | Serves 4

16 medium button mushrooms, rinsed and patted dry
70 g low-sodium salsa
3 garlic cloves, minced
1 medium onion, finely chopped
1 jalapeño pepper, minced
⅛ tsp. cayenne pepper
3 tbsps. shredded Pepper Jack cheese
2 tsps. olive oil

1. Preheat the air fryer to 180ºC.
2. Remove the stems from the mushrooms and finely chop them, reserving the whole caps.
3. In a medium bowl, mix the salsa, garlic, onion, jalapeño, cayenne, and Pepper Jack cheese. Stir in the chopped mushroom stems.
4. Stuff this mixture into the mushroom caps, mounding the filling. Drizzle the olive oil on the mushrooms. Air fry the mushrooms in the air fryer basket for 8 to 12 minutes, or until the filling is hot and the mushrooms are tender.
5. Serve immediately.

Bruschetta with Basil Pesto

Prep time: 10 minutes | Cook time: 5 to 11 minutes | Serves 4

8 slices French bread, 1-cm thick
2 tbsps. softened butter
100 g shredded Mozzarella cheese
117 g basil pesto
200 g chopped grape tomatoes
2 spring onions, thinly sliced

1. Preheat the air fryer to 180ºC.
2. Spread the bread with the butter and place butter-side up in the air fryer basket. Bake for 3 to 5 minutes, or until the bread is light golden brown.
3. Remove the bread from the basket and top each piece with some of the cheese. Return to the basket in 2 batches and bake for 1 to 3 minutes, or until the cheese melts.
4. Meanwhile, combine the pesto, tomatoes, and spring onions in a small bowl.
5. When the cheese has melted, remove the bread from the air fryer and place on a serving plate. Top each slice with some of the pesto mixture and serve.

Tortellini with Spicy Dipping Sauce

Prep time: 5 minutes | Cook time: 20 minutes | Serves 4

172 g mayonnaise
2 tbsps. mustard
1 egg
62 g flour
½ tsp. dried oregano
180 g bread crumbs
2 tbsps. olive oil
200 g frozen cheese tortellini

1. Preheat the air fryer to 190ºC.
2. In a small bowl, combine the mayonnaise and mustard and mix well. Set aside.
3. In a shallow bowl, beat the egg. In a separate bowl, combine the flour and oregano. In another bowl, combine the bread crumbs and olive oil, and mix well.
4. Drop the tortellini, a few at a time, into the egg, then into the flour, then into the egg again, and then into the bread crumbs to coat. Put into the air fryer basket, cooking in batches.
5. Air fry for about 10 minutes, shaking halfway through the cooking time, or until the tortellini are crisp and golden brown on the outside. Serve with the mayonnaise mixture.

Crispy Breaded Beef Cubes

Prep time: 10 minutes | Cook time: 12 to 16 minutes | Serves 4

454 g sirloin tip, cut into 2-cm cubes
225 g cheese pasta sauce
180 g soft bread crumbs

2 tbsps. olive oil
½ tsp. dried marjoram

1. Preheat the air fryer to 180ºC.
2. In a medium bowl, toss the beef with the pasta sauce to coat.
3. In a shallow bowl, combine the bread crumbs, oil, and marjoram, and mix well. Drop the beef cubes, one at a time, into the bread crumb mixture to coat thoroughly.
4. Air fry the beef in two batches for 6 to 8 minutes, shaking the basket once during cooking time, until the beef is at least 63ºC and the outside is crisp and brown.
5. Serve hot.

Cheesy Hash Brown Bruschetta

Prep time: 5 minutes | Cook time: 6 to 8 minutes | Serves 4

4 frozen hash browns
1 tbsp. olive oil
65 g chopped cherry tomatoes
3 tbsps. diced fresh Mozzarella

2 tbsps. grated Parmesan cheese
1 tbsp. balsamic vinegar
1 tbsp. minced fresh basil

1. Preheat the air fryer to 200ºC.
2. Place the hash brown patties in the air fryer in a single layer. Air fry for 6 to 8 minutes, or until the potatoes are crisp, hot, and golden brown.
3. Meanwhile, combine the olive oil, tomatoes, Mozzarella, Parmesan, vinegar, and basil in a small bowl.
4. When the potatoes are done, carefully remove from the basket and arrange on a serving plate. Top with the tomato mixture and serve.

Veggie Prawn Toast

Prep time: 15 minutes | Cook time: 3 to 6 minutes | Serves 4

8 large raw prawns, peeled and finely chopped
1 egg white
2 garlic cloves, minced
3 tbsps. minced red pepper
1 medium celery stalk, minced

2 tbsps. cornflour
¼ tsp. Chinese five-spice powder
3 slices firm thin-sliced no-sodium whole-wheat bread

1. Preheat the air fryer to 180ºC.
2. In a small bowl, stir together the prawns, egg white, garlic, red pepper, celery, cornflour, and five-spice powder. Top each slice of bread with one-third of the prawn mixture, spreading it evenly to the edges. With a sharp knife, cut each slice of bread into 4 strips.
3. Place the prawn toasts in the air fryer basket in a single layer. You may need to cook them in batches. Air fry for 3 to 6 minutes, until crisp and golden brown.
4. Serve hot.

Beef and Mango Skewers

Prep time: 10 minutes | Cook time: 4 to 7 minutes | Serves 4

340 g beef sirloin tip, cut into 2-cm cubes
2 tbsps. balsamic vinegar
1 tbsp. olive oil
1 tbsp. honey

½ tsp. dried marjoram
Pinch of salt
Freshly ground black pepper, to taste
1 mango

1. Preheat the air fryer to 200ºC.
2. Put the beef cubes in a medium bowl and add the balsamic vinegar, olive oil, honey, marjoram, salt, and pepper. Mix well, then massage the marinade into the beef with your hands. Set aside.
3. To prepare the mango, stand it on end and cut the skin off, using a sharp knife. Then carefully cut around the oval pit to remove the flesh. Cut the mango into 2-cm cubes.
4. Thread metal skewers alternating with three beef cubes and two mango cubes.
5. Roast the skewers in the air fryer basket for 4 to 7 minutes, or until the beef is browned and at least 65ºC.
6. Serve hot.

Buffalo Cauliflower with Sour Dip

Prep time: 10 minutes | Cook time: 10 to 14 minutes | Serves 6

1 large head cauliflower, separated into small florets
1 tbsp. olive oil
½ tsp. garlic powder
70 g low-sodium hot wing sauce, divided

171 g nonfat Greek yogurt
½ tsps. Tabasco sauce
1 celery stalk, chopped
1 tbsp. crumbled blue cheese

1. Preheat the air fryer to 190ºC.
2. In a large bowl, toss the cauliflower florets with the olive oil. Sprinkle with the garlic powder and toss again to coat. Put half of the cauliflower in the air fryer basket. Air fry for 5 to 7 minutes, or until the cauliflower is browned, shaking the basket once during cooking.
3. Transfer to a serving bowl and toss with half of the wing sauce. Repeat with the remaining cauliflower and wing sauce.
4. In a small bowl, stir together the yogurt, Tabasco sauce, celery, and blue cheese. Serve the cauliflower with the dip.

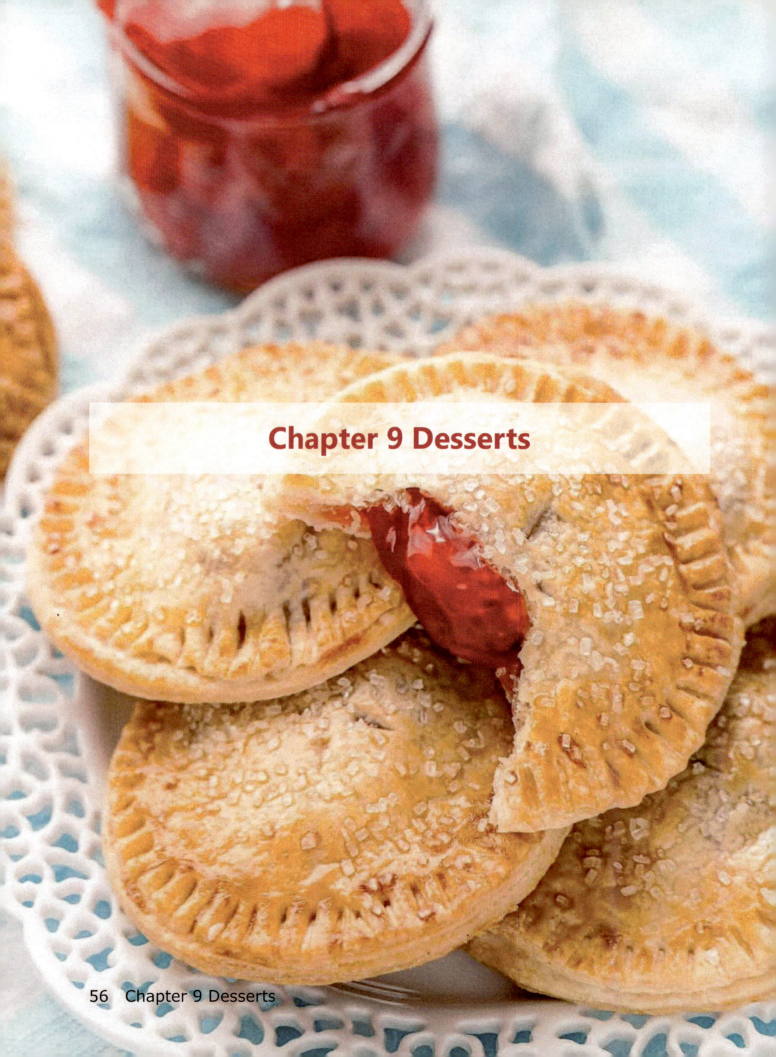

Chapter 9 Desserts

Chocolate Croissants

Prep time: 5 minutes | Cook time: 24 minutes | Serves 8

1 sheet frozen puff pastry, thawed
100 g chocolate-hazelnut spread
1 large egg, beaten

1. On a lightly floured surface, roll puff pastry into a 28-cm square. Cut pastry into quarters to form 4 squares. Cut each square diagonally to form 8 triangles.
2. Spread 2 tsps. chocolate-hazelnut spread on each triangle; from wider end, roll up pastry. Brush egg on top of each roll.
3. Preheat the air fryer to 190ºC. Air fry rolls in batches, 3 or 4 at a time, 8 minutes per batch, or until pastry is golden brown.
4. Cool on a wire rack; serve while warm or at room temperature.

Cinnamon Almonds

Prep time: 5 minutes | Cook time: 8 minutes | Serves 4

130 g whole almonds
2 tbsps. salted butter, melted
1 tbsp. sugar
½ tsp. ground cinnamon

1. Preheat the air fryer to 150ºC.
2. In a medium bowl, combine the almonds, butter, sugar, and cinnamon. Mix well to ensure all the almonds are coated with the spiced butter.
3. Transfer the almonds to the air fryer basket and shake so they are in a single layer. Bake for 8 minutes, stirring the almonds halfway through the cooking time.
4. Let cool completely before serving.

Baked Apples

Prep time: 5 minutes | Cook time: 10 minutes | Serves 4

4 small apples, cored and cut in half
2 tbsps. salted butter or coconut oil, melted
2 tbsps. sugar
1 tsp. apple pie spice
Ice cream, heavy cream, or whipped cream, for serving

1. Preheat the air fryer to 180ºC.
2. Put the apples in a large bowl. Drizzle with the melted butter and sprinkle with the sugar and apple pie spice. Use the hands to toss, ensuring the apples are evenly coated.
3. Put the apples in the air fryer basket and bake for 10 minutes. Pierce the apples with a fork to ensure they are tender.
4. Serve with ice cream, or top with a splash of heavy cream or a spoonful of whipped cream.

Pecan and Cherry Stuffed Apples

Prep time: 10 minutes | Cook time: 20 minutes | Serves 4

4 apples (about 567 g)
40 g chopped pecans
40 g dried tart cherries
1 tbsp. melted butter
3 tbsps. brown sugar
¼ tsp. allspice
Pinch salt
Ice cream, for serving

1. Cut off top 1-cm from each apple; reserve tops. With a melon baller, core through stem ends without breaking through the bottom. (Do not trim bases.)
2. Preheat the air fryer to 180ºC. Combine pecans, cherries, butter, brown sugar, allspice, and a pinch of salt. Stuff mixture into the hollow centres of the apples. Cover with apple tops. Put in the air fryer basket, using tongs. Air fry for 20 to 25 minutes, or just until tender.
3. Serve warm with ice cream.

Oatmeal and Carrot Cookie Cups

Prep time: 10 minutes | Cook time: 8 minutes | Makes 16 cups

3 tbsps. unsalted butter, at room temperature
42 g packed brown sugar
1 tbsp. honey
1 egg white
½ tsp. vanilla extract
55 g finely grated carrot
78 g quick-cooking oats
40 g whole-wheat pastry flour
½ tsp. baking soda
30 g dried cherries

1. Preheat the air fryer to 180ºC
2. In a medium bowl, beat the butter, brown sugar, and honey until well combined.
3. Add the egg white, vanilla, and carrot. Beat to combine.
4. Stir in the oats, pastry flour, and baking soda.
5. Stir in the dried cherries.
6. Double up 32 mini muffin foil cups to make 16 cups. Fill each with about 4 tsps. of dough. Bake the cookie cups, 8 at a time, for 8 minutes, or until light golden brown and just set. Serve warm.

Brazilian Pineapple Bake

Prep time: 5 minutes | Cook time: 16 minutes | Serves 4

110 g brown sugar
2 tsps. ground cinnamon
1 small pineapple, peeled, cored, and cut into

spears
3 tbsps. unsalted butter, melted

1. Preheat the air fryer to 200ºC.
2. In a small bowl, mix the brown sugar and cinnamon until thoroughly combined.
3. Brush the pineapple spears with the melted butter. Sprinkle the cinnamon-sugar over the spears, pressing lightly to ensure it adheres well.
4. Put the spears in the air fryer basket in a single layer. (Depending on the size of the air fryer, you may have to do this in batches.) Bake for 10 minutes for the first batch (6 to 8 minutes for the next batch, as the air fryer will be preheated). Halfway through the cooking time, brush the spears with butter.
5. The pineapple spears are done when they are heated through and the sugar is bubbling. Serve hot.

Cardamom and Vanilla Custard

Prep time: 5 minutes | Cook time: 25 minutes | Serves 2

240 ml whole milk
1 large egg
2 tbsps. plus 1 tsp. sugar
¼ tsp. vanilla bean paste or pure vanilla extract
¼ tsp. ground cardamom, plus more for sprinkling

1. Preheat the air fryer to 180ºC.
2. In a medium bowl, beat together the milk, egg, sugar, vanilla, and cardamom.
3. Put two ramekins in the air fryer basket. Divide the mixture between the ramekins. Sprinkle lightly with cardamom. Cover each ramekin tightly with aluminum foil. Bake for 25 minutes, or until a toothpick inserted in the centre comes out clean.
4. Let the custards cool on a wire rack for 5 to 10 minutes.
5. Serve warm, or refrigerate until cold and serve chilled.

Chapter 10 Fast and Easy Everyday Favorites

Beef Bratwursts

Prep time: 5 minutes | Cook time: 15 minutes | Serves 4

4 (85-g) beef bratwursts

1. Preheat the air fryer to 190ºC.
2. Place the beef bratwursts in the air fryer basket and air fry for 15 minutes, turning once halfway through.
3. Serve hot.

Buttery Sweet Potatoes

Prep time: 5 minutes | Cook time: 10 minutes | Serves 4

2 tbsps. butter, melted
1 tbsp. light brown sugar
2 sweet potatoes, peeled and cut into 1-cm cubes
Cooking spray

1. Preheat the air fryer to 200ºC. Line the air fryer basket with parchment paper.
2. In a medium bowl, stir together the melted butter and brown sugar until blended. Toss the sweet potatoes in the butter mixture until coated.
3. Place the sweet potatoes on the parchment and spritz with oil.
4. Air fry for 5 minutes. Shake the basket, spritz the sweet potatoes with oil, and air fry for 5 minutes more until they're soft enough to cut with a fork.
5. Serve immediately.

Corn Fritters

Prep time: 15 minutes | Cook time: 8 minutes | Serves 6

125 g self-rising flour
1 tbsp. sugar
1 tsp. salt
1 large egg, lightly beaten
56 g buttermilk
120 g corn kernels
20 g minced onion
Cooking spray

1. Preheat the air fryer to 180ºC. Line the air fryer basket with parchment paper.
2. In a medium bowl, whisk the flour, sugar, and salt until blended. Stir in the egg and buttermilk. Add the corn and minced onion. Mix well. Shape the corn fritter batter into 12 balls.
3. Place the fritters on the parchment and spritz with oil. Bake for 4 minutes. Flip the fritters, spritz them with oil, and bake for 4 minutes more until firm and lightly browned.
4. Serve immediately.

Rosemary and Orange Roasted Chickpeas

Prep time: 5 minutes | Cook time: 10 to 12 minutes | Makes 4 cups

680 g cooked chickpeas
2 tbsps. vegetable oil
1 tsp. salt
1 tsp. cumin
1 tsp. paprika
Zest of 1 orange
1 tbsp. chopped fresh rosemary

1. Preheat the air fryer to 200ºC.
2. Make sure the chickpeas are completely dry prior to roasting. In a medium bowl, toss the chickpeas with oil, salt, cumin, and paprika.
3. Working in batches, spread the chickpeas in a single layer in the air fryer basket. Air fry for 10 to 12 minutes until crisp, shaking once halfway through.
4. Return the warm chickpeas to the bowl and toss with the orange zest and rosemary. Allow to cool completely.
5. Serve.

Baked Chorizo Scotch Eggs

Prep time: 5 minutes | Cook time: 15 to 20 minutes | Makes 4 eggs

454 g Mexican chorizo or other seasoned sausage meat
4 soft-boiled eggs plus 1 raw egg
1 tbsp. water
60 g plain flour
120 g panko bread crumbs
Cooking spray

1. Divide the chorizo into 4 equal portions. Flatten each portion into a disc. Place a soft-boiled egg in the centre of each disc. Wrap the chorizo around the egg, encasing it completely. Place the encased eggs on a plate and chill for at least 30 minutes.
2. Preheat the air fryer to 180ºC.
3. Beat the raw egg with 1 tbsp. of water. Place the flour on a small plate and the panko on a second plate. Working with 1 egg at a time, roll the encased egg in the flour, then dip it in the egg mixture. Dredge the egg in the panko and place on a plate. Repeat with the remaining eggs.
4. Spray the eggs with oil and place in the air fryer basket. Bake for 10 minutes. Turn and bake for an additional 5 to 10 minutes, or until browned and crisp on all sides.
5. Serve immediately.

Easy Roasted Asparagus

Prep time: 5 minutes | Cook time: 6 minutes | Serves 4

454 g asparagus, trimmed and halved crosswise
1 tsp. extra-virgin olive oil
Salt and pepper, to taste
Lemon wedges, for serving

1. Preheat the air fryer to 200ºC.
2. Toss the asparagus with the oil, ⅛ tsp. salt, and ⅛ tsp. pepper in bowl. Transfer to air fryer basket.
3. Place the basket in air fryer and roast for 6 to 8 minutes, or until tender and bright green, tossing halfway through cooking.
4. Season with salt and pepper and serve with lemon wedges.

Indian-Style Sweet Potato Fries

Prep time: 5 minutes | Cook time: 8 minutes | Makes 20 fries

Seasoning Mixture:
¾ tsp. ground coriander
½ tsp. garam masala
½ tsp. garlic powder
½ tsp. ground cumin

¼ tsp. ground cayenne pepper
Fries:
2 large sweet potatoes, peeled
2 tsps. olive oil

1. Preheat the air fryer to 200ºC.
2. In a small bowl, combine the coriander, garam masala, garlic powder, cumin, and cayenne pepper.
3. Slice the sweet potatoes into ½-cm thick fries.
4. In a large bowl, toss the sliced sweet potatoes with the olive oil and the seasoning mixture.
5. Transfer the seasoned sweet potatoes to the air fryer basket and fry for 8 minutes, until crispy.
6. Serve warm.

Pomegranate Avocado Fries

Prep time: 5 minutes | Cook time: 7 to 8 minutes | Serves 4

120 g panko bread crumbs
1 tsp. salt, plus more for sprinkling
1 tsp. garlic powder
½ tsp. cayenne pepper

2 ripe but firm avocados
1 egg, beaten with 1 tbsp. water
Cooking spraying
Pomegranate molasses, for serving

1. Preheat the air fryer to 190ºC.
2. Whisk together the panko, salt, and spices on a plate. Cut each avocado in half and remove the pit. Cut each avocado half into 4 slices and scoop the slices out with a large spoon, taking care to keep the slices intact.
3. Dip each avocado slice in the egg wash and then dredge it in the panko. Place the breaded avocado slices on a plate.
4. Working in 2 batches, arrange half of the avocado slices in a single layer in the air fryer basket. Spray lightly with oil. Bake the slices for 7 to 8 minutes, turning once halfway through. Remove the cooked slices to a platter and repeat with the remaining avocado slices.
5. Sprinkle the warm avocado slices with salt and drizzle with pomegranate molasses. Serve immediately.

Gold Ravioli

Prep time: 10 minutes | Cook time: 6 minutes | Serves 4

60 g panko bread crumbs
2 tsps. nutritional yeast
1 tsp. dried basil
1 tsp. dried oregano
1 tsp. garlic powder

Salt and ground black pepper, to taste
60 ml chickpea water
227 g ravioli
Cooking spray

1. Cover the air fryer basket with aluminum foil and coat with a light brushing of oil.
2. Preheat the air fryer to 200ºC. Combine the panko bread crumbs, nutritional yeast, basil, oregano, and garlic powder. Sprinkle with salt and pepper to taste.
3. Put the chickpea water in a separate bowl. Dip the ravioli in the chickpea water before coating it in the panko mixture. Spritz with cooking spray and transfer to the air fryer.
4. Air fry for 6 minutes. Shake the air fryer basket halfway.
5. Serve hot.

Appendix 1: Measurement Conversion Chart

Volume Equivalents (Dry)

US STANDARD	METRIC (APPROXIMATE)
1/8 teaspoon	0.5 mL
1/4 teaspoon	1 mL
1/2 teaspoon	2 mL
3/4 teaspoon	4 mL
1 teaspoon	5 mL
1 tablespoon	15 mL
1/4 cup	59 mL
1/2 cup	118 mL
3/4 cup	177 mL
1 cup	235 mL
2 cups	475 mL
3 cups	700 mL
4 cups	1 L

Temperatures Equivalents

FAHRENHEIT (F)	CELSIUS(C) (APPROXIMATE)
225 °F	107 °C
250 °F	120 °C
275 °F	135 °C
300 °F	150 °C
325 °F	160 °C
350 °F	180 °C
375 °F	190 °C
400 °F	205 °C
425 °F	220 °C
450 °F	235 °C
475 °F	245 °C
500 °F	260 °C

Volume Equivalents (Liquid)

US STANDARD	US STANDARD (OUNCES)	METRIC (APPROXIMATE)
2 tablespoons	1 fl.oz.	30 mL
1/4 cup	2 fl.oz.	60 mL
1/2 cup	4 fl.oz.	120 mL
1 cup	8 fl.oz.	240 mL
1 1/2 cup	12 fl.oz.	355 mL
2 cups or 1 pint	16 fl.oz.	475 mL
4 cups or 1 quart	32 fl.oz.	1 L
1 gallon	128 fl.oz.	4 L

Weight Equivalents

US STANDARD	METRIC (APPROXIMATE)
1 ounce	28 g
2 ounces	57 g
5 ounces	142 g
10 ounces	284 g
15 ounces	425 g
16 ounces (1 pound)	455 g
1.5 pounds	680 g
2 pounds	907 g

Appendix 2: Air Fryer Time Table

Beef

Item	Temp (°F)	Time (mins)	Item	Temp (°F)	Time (mins)
Beef Eye Round Roast (4 lbs.)	400 °F	45 to 55	Meatballs (1-inch)	370 °F	7
Burger Patty (4 oz.)	370 °F	16 to 20	Meatballs (3-inch)	380 °F	10
Filet Mignon (8 oz.)	400 °F	18	Ribeye, bone-in (1-inch, 8 oz)	400 °F	10 to 15
Flank Steak (1.5 lbs.)	400 °F	12	Sirloin steaks (1-inch, 12 oz)	400 °F	9 to 14
Flank Steak (2 lbs.)	400 °F	20 to 28			

Chicken

Item	Temp (°F)	Time (mins)	Item	Temp (°F)	Time (mins)
Breasts, bone in (1 ¼ lb.)	370 °F	25	Legs, bone-in (1 ¾ lb.)	380 °F	30
Breasts, boneless (4 oz)	380 °F	12	Thighs, boneless (1 ½ lb.)	380 °F	18 to 20
Drumsticks (2 ½ lb.)	370 °F	20	Wings (2 lb.)	400 °F	12
Game Hen (halved 2 lb.)	390 °F	20	Whole Chicken	360 °F	75
Thighs, bone-in (2 lb.)	380 °F	22	Tenders	360 °F	8 to 10

Pork & Lamb

Item	Temp (°F)	Time (mins)	Item	Temp (°F)	Time (mins)
Bacon (regular)	400 °F	5 to 7	Pork Tenderloin	370 °F	15
Bacon (thick cut)	400 °F	6 to 10	Sausages	380 °F	15
Pork Loin (2 lb.)	360 °F	55	Lamb Loin Chops (1-inch thick)	400 °F	8 to 12
Pork Chops, bone in (1-inch, 6.5 oz)	400 °F	12	Rack of Lamb (1.5 – 2 lb.)	380 °F	22

Fish & Seafood

Item	Temp (°F)	Time (mins)	Item	Temp (°F)	Time (mins)
Calamari (8 oz)	400 °F	4	Tuna Steak	400 °F	7 to 10
Fish Fillet (1-inch, 8 oz)	400 °F	10	Scallops	400 °F	5 to 7
Salmon, fillet (6 oz)	380 °F	12	Shrimp	400 °F	5
Swordfish steak	400 °F	10			

Vegetables

INGREDIENT	AMOUNT	PREPARATION	OIL	TEMP	COOK TIME
Asparagus	2 bunches	Cut in half, trim stems	2 Tbsp	420°F	12-15 mins
Beets	1½ lbs	Peel, cut in ½-inch cubes	1Tbsp	390°F	28-30 mins
Bell peppers (for roasting)	4 peppers	Cut in quarters, remove seeds	1Tbsp	400°F	15-20 mins
Broccoli	1 large head	Cut in 1-2-inch florets	1Tbsp	400°F	15-20 mins
Brussels sprouts	1lb	Cut in half, remove stems	1Tbsp	425°F	15-20 mins
Carrots	1lb	Peel, cut in ¼-inch rounds	1 Tbsp	425°F	10-15 mins
Cauliflower	1 head	Cut in 1-2-inch florets	2 Tbsp	400°F	20-22 mins
Corn on the cob	7 ears	Whole ears, remove husks	1Tbsp	400°F	14-17 mins
Green beans	1 bag (12 oz)	Trim	1Tbsp	420°F	18-20 mins
Kale (for chips)	4 oz	Tear into pieces,remove stems	None	325°F	5-8 mins
Mushrooms	16 oz	Rinse, slice thinly	1Tbsp	390°F	25-30 mins
Potatoes, russet	1½ lbs	Cut in 1-inch wedges	1Tbsp	390°F	25-30 mins
Potatoes, russet	1lb	Hand-cut fries, soak 30 mins in cold water, then pat dry	½ -3 Tbsp	400°F	25-28 mins
Potatoes, sweet	1lb	Hand-cut fries, soak 30 mins in cold water, then pat dry	1Tbsp	400°F	25-28 mins
Zucchini	1lb	Cut in eighths lengthwise, then cut in half	1Tbsp	400°F	15-20 mins

Appendix 3: Recipes Index

Dear Readers,

We are glad that you purchased this book, your opinion is very important to us. If you have any comments and suggestions on this cookbook, we sincerely invite you to send us an email for feedback.

With your participation, we will grow faster and better.

After receiving your email, we will upgrade the product according to your needs and give you an e-book of 50 recipes as a gift.

We are committed to continuous growth and progress, providing readers with cookbooks that help create a better kitchen life and a healthy body.

I wish you happy every day.

Company contact email: Healthrecipegroup@outlook.com

Printed in Great Britain
by Amazon

13158215R00045